Calvin's Doctrine of the State

Calvin's Doctrine of the State

*A Reformed Doctrine and Its American Trajectory,
The Revolutionary War, and the Founding
of the Republic*

MARK J. LARSON

WIPF & STOCK · Eugene, Oregon

CALVIN'S DOCTRINE OF THE STATE
A Reformed Doctrine and Its American Trajectory, The
Revolutionary War, and the Founding of the Republic

Copyright © 2009 Mark J. Larson. All rights reserved. Except for brief quotations in critical publications or reviews, no part of this book may be reproduced in any manner without prior written permission from the publisher. Write: Permissions, Wipf and Stock Publishers, 199 W. 8th Ave., Suite 3, Eugene, OR 97401.

Wipf & Stock
A Division of Wipf and Stock Publishers
199 W. 8th Ave., Suite 3
Eugene, OR 97401

www.wipfandstock.com

ISBN 13: 978-1-60608-073-3

Manufactured in the U.S.A.

For my children

Contents

Preface ix
Abbreviations xi
Introduction xiii

1 The Question of Theocracy 1

2 The Making of War 20

3 Godly Warfare 34

4 Warring by the Popular Magistrates 52

5 The Justice of War 66

6 Political Legacy 81

Conclusion 101
Bibliography 105
Subject/Name Index 127

Preface

I AM thankful for a host of professors who through the years piqued my interest in history and political philosophy. Among the greatest of them was James McGoldrick, my distinguished professor of history from my days at Cedarville University. Other scholars who made a deep impression upon me were Rembert Carter, Sam Logan, and Gregg Singer. I am thankful for each of them. Robert Kingdon at the University of Wisconsin, by way of example, showed me how to teach with kindness and civility. I owe much to Richard Gamble—the very first Calvin scholar I ever met—from my student days at Westminster Theological Seminary. I am thankful for Douglas Kelly, whose writing first directed my attention to Calvin and his political theory. An enormous debt of gratitude is owed to Richard Muller—my doctoral adviser at Calvin Theological Seminary—who exemplifies greatness as a theologian and a historian. His penetrating analysis, great humor, and good common sense will always be appreciated.

Let me also express my high regard for the editors at Wipf and Stock Publishers. Their expertise has made it possible for this volume to be published in the five-hundred-year anniversary of the birth of John Calvin. It has been a pleasure to work with such a professional and courteous staff.

The topics examined in this volume compel me to remember with honor a brave and yet humble Marine—my father-in-law, Dan Kimberlin. He took up arms in the Second World War in the South Pacific in the defense of freedom. This was the very thing that Calvin sanctioned in his doctrine of political ethics as being just in the sight of God. I likewise express my thanks to my own parents. My mother put within me a desire for scholarship. My father gave me a love of history and a fascination with politics. His love of liberty and republicanism is now my own. May I be able to transmit the values of the American constitutional experiment to the next generation. Unto that end I dedicate this book to my own children with love and affection. At the same time I ever thank God for their mother, my faithful wife and helper. Apart from her, this book would not have been possible.

Abbreviations

ARH	*Archive for Reformation History*
AUSS	*Andrews University Seminary Studies*
BHR	*Bibliothèque D' Humanisme Et Renaissance*
BLT	*Brethren Life and Thought*
BS	*Bibliotheca Sacra*
BSJAG	*Bulletin de la Société d' Histoirie et d'Archéologie de Genève*
CH	*Church History*
CTJ	*Calvin Theological Journal*
CTM	*Concordia Theological Monthly*
DRCH	*Dutch Review of Church History*
EQ	*Evangelical Quarterly*
JEH	*Journal of Ecclesiastical History*
JLPS	*Journal of Law and Political Studies*
JPG	*Journal of Presbyterian History*
IRB	*International Reformed Bulletin*
PL	*Positions Lutheriennes*
PTR	*Pacific Theological Review*
RP	*The Review of Politics*
RTP	*Revue de Thaeologie et de Philosophie*
RTR	*The Reformed Theological Review*
SBET	*The Scottish Bulletin of Evangelical Theology*
SBT	*Studia Biblia et Theologica*
SJT	*Scottish Journal of Theology*
TT	*Theology Today*
WTJ	*The Westminster Theological Journal*

Introduction

"No one ought to doubt that civil authority is a calling, not only holy and lawful before God, but also the most sacred and by far the most honorable of all callings in the whole life of mortal men."[1] For the sake of the maintenance of humanity and the protection of the Christian religion, civil government has an indispensable place: "Its function among men is no less than that of bread, water, sun, and air; indeed, its place of honor is far more excellent."[2] In these declarations John Calvin reflected something of his profound appreciation for civil government and his intense political interest. He had without a doubt a "deep and abiding interest in the affairs of state."[3] It was more, though, than the simple fact that Calvin enjoyed dabbling in political reflection. He was an astute political philosopher.[4] Calvin's writings on the subject of political doctrine made available to the church a "biblical frame of reference" for its thinking on political issues.[5] There is no question that he developed his political thought in connection with his exegetical interaction with the Scripture. Important constituent elements that make

---

1. Calvin, *Institutes*, IV.20.4. Unless otherwise indicated, all references to the *Institutes* are from the Battles' translation.
2. *Institutes* IV.20.3.
3. Singer, *John Calvin*, 33.
4. Oberman, "*Europa afflicta*," 107.
5. Singer, "Calvin and the Social Order," 230–31.

up a Reformed political philosophy in our day likewise trace their lineage back to Calvin.[6]

Contemporary treatments of the political views of Calvin, however, often imply that he was a bellicose autocrat—a harsh man who tyrannized Geneva in the context of a theocratic government and who entertained the idea of holy war against hostile powers. They contend that the pastor, indeed the jurist, who wrote the constitutions of both church and state in Geneva was committed to theocracy as a form of government. The theologian who wrote about God and war embraced holy war ideology. For some scholars, Calvin was one or both of the above—so that these categories of theocracy and holy war are viewed as interrelated in discussions of Calvin's politics.

Against such an interpretation of Calvin the theocrat and holy war advocate, I shall argue on the basis of a careful examination of his theological production—particularly the *Institutes*, biblical commentaries, and sermons—that Calvin favored a republican civil polity and that he positioned himself in the mainstream of the medieval just war tradition that arose from the foundational teaching of Augustine of Hippo. His preference for a mixed government with aristocratic and democratic elements reflects his fear of autocracy. He insisted that when there is a monarchy in a nation, the popular magistrates must provide an institutional check upon tyrannical kings who might arise. Warfare initiated by such parliamentary bodies was to be conducted in terms of the medieval just war tradition and its commitment both to the justice of war and justice in war.

The door to holy war thinking—which some Puritans embraced in the seventeenth century, seen in a theologian like William Gouge—was not opened by Calvin or his associate Theodore Beza. The seeds of holy war doctrine among the

---

6. Spykman, "The Principled Pluralist Position," 83–85.

English Reformed are to be found in the teaching of the Zurich theologians Henry Bullinger and Peter Martyr Vermigli. Calvin remained conservative to the very end of his life.

An examination of the several genre where Calvin treated the doctrine of the state and war must be conducted against the background of the Augustinian just war tradition. Calvin did not create his theology out of a vacuum. He had great respect for the doctrinal tradition of the Christian church—even while he subjected certain aspects of it to intense criticism on the basis of his understanding of the biblical standard—and he used it in sharpening his understanding of the Christian faith. It is indeed manifest that Calvin stands in continuity with the major thinkers on the subject of the just war. His writings manifest substantial and fundamental agreement with Augustine's war doctrine as expressed in *Reply to Faustus the Manichean* and with Aquinas' discussion on war in *Summa Theologica*. Fundamental perspectives of Isidore of Seville articulated in *Etymologiae* and in *Policraticus* by John of Salisbury are repeated in Calvin's political philosophy.

The dominant impression that Calvin casts is one of conservatism.[7] This is the case even though he repudiated numerous entrenched teachings of Roman Catholic theology, particularly as they related to the doctrine of salvation and the doctrine of the church and sacraments. He likewise rejected the longstanding preference of most political thinkers for monarchy. Calvin still nevertheless appears distinctively medieval and traditional on matters relative to political ethics—and not by any means strikingly original, although he did dissent from Augustine on the meaning of certain biblical texts, such as Luke 22:35–38.[8]

7. Heller, *The Conquest of Poverty*, 111.

8. In this intriguing passage of scripture, Jesus speaks to his disciples and declares that the person who has no sword is to sell his coat and buy one. Augustine of Hippo, in *Reply to Faustus the Manichaean* XXII.77,

Calvin was not a radical thinker on war. Even his doctrine of resistance by the popular magistrates had antecedents in the medieval political tradition.

Calvin must also be examined in the context of the teaching of his contemporaries. There is continuity between Calvin and Luther. This itself is significant because everyone agrees that the German reformer stood in the just war tradition, being adamantly opposed to the holy war idea.[9] Luther's relevant works are *On Secular Authority* (1523), *Against the Robbing and Murdering Hordes of Peasants* (1525), *Whether Soldiers, Too, Can Be Saved* (1526), *On War against the Turk* (1529), and *Dr Martin Luther's Warning to His Dear German People* (1531).

Within the Reformed tradition, the major theologians considered in this study along with Calvin are Henry Bullinger (the *Decades*, Sermons 6–9 of the second decade), Peter Martyr Vermigli (*The Common Places* IV.17), and Theodore Beza (*Concerning the Rights of Rulers*). Each of these biblical scholars was fairly close to Calvin in age. While Calvin was born in 1509, Vermigli was born in 1499, Bullinger in 1504, and Beza in 1519. Each man had a strong interest in political philosophy. Each one labored in the geographical context of the Swiss Reformation. By demarcating the parameters of this study in such a way we gain the additional advantage of being able to examine theologians who came from two different approaches within the Reformed tradition on the matter of church and state. Calvin and Beza were committed to the two-sphere struc-

---

insisted upon a literal interpretation of Christ's directive. Calvin, though, argued that the command of Jesus should be understood figuratively. For Calvin, Jesus was using metaphorical language to indicate that the apostles needed to be well-armed with spiritual weapons. See *Commentary on a Harmony of the Evangelists*, 222–23.

9. Ramsey, *War and the Christian Conscience*, 116–17; Johnson, *The Quest for Peace*, 145; Miller, "Fighting Like a Christian," 44.

ture of Genevan Presbyterianism, in which pastors and elders governed the church.[10] Bullinger, on the other hand, espoused the one-sphere doctrine of Erastianism—an approach in which the civil magistrates fully governed the church, a structure in which Vermigli was willing to participate.

The advantage of a contextual approach is that it casts an important perspective upon Calvin. He provided the most conservative doctrine on the just war among the dominant Reformed theologians of his time in Geneva and Zurich. It was Calvin, in contrast with Bullinger and Vermigli, who kept the door closed against holy war policy. It was Calvin, in contrast with Beza (who allowed the assassination of a usurping tyrant by a private citizen), who always insisted that resistance by arms must only be initiated by the proper civil authority.

The foundation of Reformed political thought that Calvin laid in the sixteenth century is discussed with the following structure in view. The first half of the book demonstrates that Calvin did not teach a theocratic civil polity (chapter one) and that he did not believe in holy war—a war authorized by the church and a war that is prosecuted without restraint. Civil government alone has the authority to wage war (chapter two), and the waging of war must be done with humanity and restraint (chapter three). The second half of the volume lays out what Calvin actually did believe on the doctrine of the state and war. Chapter four presents his teaching regarding parliamentary resistance against monarchical tyranny. Chapter five expounds upon his commitment to the just war categories of just cause, right intention, and last resort. Chapter six reflects upon his political legacy in the American Revolutionary War and in the constitutional determination for a republic in these United States.

---

10. Larson, "John Calvin and Genevan Presbyterianism," 43–69; Maruyama, *The Ecclesiology of Theodore Beza*.

I

The Question of Theocracy

"CHRIST WISHED to bar the ministers of his Word from civil rule and earthly authority." Calvin indeed went on to say, "The office of pastor is distinct from that of prince," and the two "are so different that they cannot come together in one man."[1] Despite such clear statements in which he forcefully rejected the concept of a theocratic government, elements of older and even more recent scholarship contend that Calvin deliberately implemented a theocratic structure in which he and his fellow pastors took control of the Republic of Geneva.[2] According to this popular and stereotypical presentation,[3] as head of the Genevan state, Calvin was able to initiate a moral reign of terror.[4]

1. *Institutes* IV.11.8.
2. The term *theocracy* refers to a state which is governed by the clergy. See Walton, *Zwingli's Theocracy*, 1.
3. Olson, "A Response to 'Calvin's Socio-Political Legacy,'" 124, refers to "the stereotype that still exists of Geneva as a theocracy under the thumb of Calvin." She maintains that "Calvin was not an absolutist" and did not favor "rule by one person."
4. Allen, as representative of the older scholarship, affirms in *A History of Political Thought in the Sixteenth Century*, 64, "Calvin made of the ministers, acting as a body, and the Consistory they dominated, the real masters of Geneva." In contemporary scholarship, McGrath, *Reformation Thought*, 216, refers to "the Genevan theocracy." Collinson, *The Reformation*, 81, likewise regards Geneva as a "creeping theocracy."

What actually happened in Geneva in the time of the Reformation? Was it the intention of Calvin to establish a theocracy in which he in particular would wield autocratic authority over both church and state?[5] An examination of the church constitution that he himself drafted—the *Ecclesiastical Ordinances* of 1541—demonstrates that Calvin intended to establish neither a theocracy nor an autocracy.[6]

THE DOCTRINE OF TWO SPHERES

The fact of the matter is that Calvin believed in a separation of church and state in terms of their respective jurisdictions.[7] He embraced the position that there are *two spheres*—the civil and the ecclesiastical, the church having control over Christian discipline. This two-sphere doctrine meant that Calvin and the other pastors in Geneva would have no political authority.[8] Whatever

---

5. At the foundation of the reform in Geneva was the elimination of one-man rule. Kingdon, "International Calvinism," 231, makes the point that the Genevan Reformation entailed the removal of ecclesiastical monarchicalism: "All traces of the one-man rule associated with the Catholic institution of bishop were to be abolished." Cf. Kingdon, "Calvin and 'Presbytery': the Geneva Company of Pastors," 43.

6. Oberman, "John Calvin: The Mystery of His Impact," 2, calls attention to the vital significance of the *Ecclesiastical Ordinances* and also the consistory and later the Academy of Geneva: "Without these structural underpinnings of Calvin's heritage his *Institutio* . . . would not have become the textbook of so many Reformed theologians of his day—let alone of later days!" Cf. Harbison, *The Age of Reformation*, 76.

7. Witte, *Religion and the American Constitutional Experiment*, 23. Cf. Raath, "Covenant and the Christian Community," 1006.

8. Theodore Beza, who followed Calvin as the moderator of the Company of Pastors, suggested that there was nothing inherently wrong with one man holding two offices. In his treatise *Concerning the Rights of Rulers over Their Subjects and the Duty of Subjects towards Their Rulers*, 83, Beza cited from the Bible Melchizedek who was both the king of

power they had would be restricted to the ecclesiastical sphere alone.⁹ Far from establishing a theocracy in which Calvin and the ministers ruled the city, Calvin and his colleagues had to "fight step-by-step to maintain the autonomy of the church against the ascendancy of the councils" of the civil government of Geneva.¹⁰

Calvin, in other words, rejected one of the doctrines of the medieval church—the theory that regalian bishops (bishops who possessed the "regalia" of secular office) possessed both a religious and a secular sword. Martin Luther was renowned for his expressions of outrage concerning this medieval doctrine that entailed the use of the temporal sword by the clergy. "The pope and the bishops," he insisted, "would be deserting their calling and office to fight with sword against flesh and blood." Luther stated in no uncertain terms, "They are not commanded to do this; it is forbidden."¹¹ Here we must recognize that Calvin was no less adamant in his repudiation of this theory.

The canon lawyers had based their claim upon an allegorical interpretation of Luke 22:38, a text in which the apostles

---

Salem and the priest of God Most High. The possession of a civil and an ecclesiastical office in the case of Melchizedek, Beza maintained, shows that "these two offices" are not "incompatible with each other." The reason why these offices "were afterwards separated by the Lord," said Beza, is "because one man could scarcely be equal to the performance of both." A more recent translation of Beza is provided by Franklin, *Right of Magistrates*, in *Constitutionalism and Resistance in the Sixteenth Century*, 101–35. Franklin's translation is more readable, although it is highly abridged. All English references to Beza in this volume are to the Gonin translation.

9. Höpfl, in *Luther and Calvin on Secular Authority*, xlvi, properly recognizes that "a satisfactory understanding of Calvin's political thought demands attention to his ecclesiastical thought."

10. Cottret, *Calvin*, 159, 164.

11. *On War against the Turk*, 165.

directed the attention of Jesus to two swords.[12] In the passage Christ responded by saying that the two swords were enough. In his biblical commentary on this text, Calvin wrote, "As to the inference which the Doctors of Canon Law draw from these words—that their mitred bishops have a double jurisdiction—it is not only an offensive allegory, but a detestable mockery, by which they ridicule the word of God."[13]

In order to underscore the validity of this contention—that Calvin believed in a two-sphere structure for the Christian commonwealth—we need to consider some of the specifics of his teaching in the *Ecclesiastical Ordinances*.[14] A fundamental point of the constitution Calvin provided for the church in Geneva was that the consistory had a limited, spiritual jurisdiction, while the magistrates retained their civil authority in the Republic.[15]

A careful study of the church constitution makes it clear that Calvin viewed the consistory as being a church court and not a civil one.[16] Its jurisdiction was ecclesiastical, rather than

---

12. The doctrine of the regalian bishop as based upon Luke 22:38 is a variation on the two-swords theory as articulated by Pope Boniface VIII. See his bull *Unam Sanctum* of 1302 in Bettenson, *Documents of the Christian Church*, 115–16.

13. *Commentary on a Harmony of the Evangelists*, 224.

14. A good English translation of Calvin's *Ordonnances Ecclésiastiques* is provided in *The Register of the Company of Pastors of Geneva in the Time of Calvin*. The original French version is in *Registres de la Compagnie des Pasteurs de Genève au temps de Calvin*. The *Ecclesiastical Ordinances* of 1541 were twice revised in the sixteenth century—in 1561 and once again in 1576.

15. The fact that the consistory had a spiritual concern does not mean that it was only concerned with matters relating to personal ethics. Social ethics were also an issue of interest to the pastors and elders of Geneva. Chadwick, *The Reformation*, 86.

16. Although Calvin did not originate every aspect of his church polity—Johannes Oecolampadius first insisted upon ecclesiastical rather

civil.[17] This point is made at the very end of the document: "All this is to be done in such a way that the ministers have no jurisdiction and wield only the spiritual sword of the Word of God . . . and that there is no derogation by this consistory from the authority of the Seigneury or the magistracy; but the civil power shall continue in its entirety."[18]

The fact that the Geneva consistory was a church court with a limited, spiritual jurisdiction is seen in the type of cases that came before it.[19] A parishioner would find himself or herself

---

than magisterial discipline and Martin Bucer first developed a doctrine of four ecclesiastical offices—it seems quite evident that it was the form of church government that Calvin established in Geneva in terms of its fundamental constituents that spread throughout the world—going to France, Scotland, Holland, Hungary, and elsewhere. Cf. Labrousse, *Bayle*, 3; Kingdon, "Calvin's Socio-Political Legacy: Collective Government, Resistance to Tyranny, Discipline," 114.

17. Roget, *L'Église et l'État à Genève du temps de Calvin*, 31.

18. *Ecclesiastical Ordinances*, 49.

19. Calvin's commitment to *ecclesiastical* discipline, rather than *magisterial* discipline, was in itself a defining characteristic of his version of the Reformed faith. Calvin's emphasis upon discipline by church leaders distinguished him from many of the ministers who were in Geneva when he returned in 1541. Many of them believed that Calvin's approach was usurping power that really belonged to the civil government. Calvin's beliefs in this area also distinguished him from most of the other Protestant reformers who were convinced that the civil magistrate alone had the power to discipline. This Erastian conception was embraced by Zwingli and Bullinger in Zurich. In Lutheran countries the right to discipline was likewise retained by civil governments. The disciplinary work of the consistory may be examined firsthand in the *Registers of the Consistory of Geneva in the Time of Calvin*, 1:1542–44. The consistory records for 1545–46 are now available in *Registres du Consistoire de Genève au Temps de Calvin*, Tome 2. The consistory records for 1547–48 are likewise available in *Registres du Consistoire de Genève au Temps de Calvin*. Köhler, *Zürcher Ehegericht und Genfer Konsistorium,* deals with magisterial

before the consistory because of either a doctrinal or behavioral problem.[20] The *Ecclesiastical Ordinances* refer to the possibility of a doctrinal aberration and make the assumption that such a case belongs to the jurisdiction of the consistory: "If anyone speaks critically against the received doctrine, he shall be summoned for the purpose of reasoning with him."[21] As to problematic behavior, the church constitution provides two specific examples which the consistory would respond to because they fall into the category of a spiritual issue: "If anyone is negligent to come to church in such a way that serious contempt of the communion of Christians is apparent, or if anyone shows himself to be scornful of ecclesiastical rule, he shall be admonished."[22] Both of these examples may be classified as "religious" behavioral problems.[23]

The consistory in the time of Calvin was also committed to dealing with "moral" behavioral problems. The consistory registers show that the spiritual jurisdiction of the consistory embraced such moral aberrations as vandalism, stealing, lying, sexual misconduct, domestic quarrels, and many other sins as well.[24]

The two-sphere doctrine of Calvin is seen in the limited jurisdiction of the consistory, as its responsibilities are positively spelled out in the *Ecclesiastical Ordinances*. His teaching on the two spheres is also presented in two more ways. First, the church constitution insisted that "the ministers have no civil jurisdiction and wield only the spiritual sword of the Word of God."[25] It must never be forgotten that Calvin and the rest of the consis-

---

discipline in Zurich at length.

20. Walker, *John Calvin*, 274.
21. *Ecclesiastical Ordinances*, 48.
22. Ibid.
23. Kingdon, "The Control of Morals in Calvin's Geneva," 9.
24. Monter, "The Consistory of Geneva," 467–84.
25. *Ecclesiastical Ordinances*, 49.

tory never put a single heretic (including Michael Servetus), a single murderer, or a single adulterer to death.[26] They may well have concurred with a particular execution, but it was the Small Council alone which had the power of the supreme penalty of capital punishment. Secondly, the constitution of the church not only specified what the consistory could not do, but it also buttressed the already established powers of the civil rulers: "There is no derogation by this consistory from the authority of the Seigneury or the magistracy; but the civil power shall continue in its entirety."[27]

This specified limitation upon the power of the consistory—this separation between the jurisdiction of the ministers and the jurisdiction of the magistrates—was in sharp contrast to the previous history of Geneva when it was ruled autocratically for centuries by a prince-bishop who possessed both civil and ecclesiastical jurisdiction. Calvin's structure, which distinguished between church government and civil government, was also in marked contrast to the arrangement that had long prevailed in Rome, in which the Pope was both the head of the church and the temporal prince of the Papal States. Calvin in no sense was the Pope of Geneva.[28]

ORDAINED TO TEACH

The fact that pastors had no civil jurisdiction in the teaching of Calvin is underscored by examining his reflections on pastoral

---

26. *Adultery and Divorce in Calvin's Geneva*, 118–19.

27. *Ecclesiastical Ordinances*, 49.

28. Chenevière, "Did Calvin Advocate Theocracy?" 160, states that Calvin "never showed the least sympathy for theocracy" and that he engaged in "constant criticism of the Roman clergy for usurping the temporal power of princes."

theology.[29] He had a well-developed conception as to the responsibilities of the pastoral office, articulated in terms of a three-fold function: "With regard to pastors . . . their office is to proclaim the Word of God for the purpose of instructing, admonishing, exhorting, and reproving . . . to administer the sacraments, and to exercise fraternal discipline together with the elders."[30] Calvin never wavered from this perspective regarding what the pastor was called to do. The 1559 *Institutes* surfaces the same position. "Pastors . . . have been set over the church," he contended, "to instruct the people to true godliness, to administer the sacred mysteries and to keep and exercise upright discipline."[31]

With respect to these three functions, Calvin had the most to say about teaching.[32] The reason, no doubt, for this emphasis was his belief that the pastor is "elected principally for the sake of teaching."[33] Ministers, quite simply, are "ordained to teach."[34] "The ministry of pastors" was "to administer" the Scripture, "which is the duty enjoined upon them."[35] It has been correctly stated that for Calvin "the basic and fundamental character of the pastoral ministry is the proclamation of the gospel."[36] At this point he stood in total continuity with Luther who argued that

---

29. As Armstrong has noted, "The Pastoral Office in Calvin," 157, additional scholarly attention needs to be given to Calvin's pastoral doctrine.

30. *Ecclesiastical Ordinances*, 36.

31. *Institutes* IV.3.6.

32. Taylor, "John Calvin, the Teacher," 128–29.

33. Calvin, *Commentaries on the Epistle to Titus*, 295.

34. Calvin, *Commentaries on the First Epistle to Timothy*, 138.

35. Calvin, *Commentaries on the Second Epistle to Timothy*, 252.

36. Reid, "John Calvin, Pastoral Theologian," 68.

the bishops of the church must give themselves to their calling, to pastor the flock of God, to preach the word of God.[37]

Who was the good pastor in the view of Calvin? It was the man who was "diligent in teaching."[38] Of course, that which was to be taught was nothing less than Scripture itself: "Let the ministers of churches faithfully attend to the ministry of the Word, not adulterating the teaching of salvation, but delivering it pure and undefiled to God's people."[39]

In his farewell to the ministers of Geneva (on April 28, 1564) we find Calvin's self-assessment of his own work of teaching the Bible: "As to my doctrine, I have taught faithfully, and God has given me grace to write what I have written as faithfully as it was in my power. I have not falsified a single passage of the Scriptures, nor given it a wrong interpretation to the best of my knowledge."[40]

It is quite clear that Calvin believed that the ordination of the pastor to teach meant that he had the responsibility to study. This was a duty from which Calvin did not shrink, keeping long hours in his study.[41] It was his position that study was a pastoral imperative: "All godly teachers . . . must indeed study diligently, so as not to ascend the pulpit till they have been fully prepared."[42] He asked, "How shall pastors teach others if they be not eager to learn?"[43]

The pastor's overall objective in his teaching should be to bring consolation, "to comfort the people of God by the gospel

---

37. *On War against the Turk*, 165–67.
38. *Commentaries on the First Epistle to Timothy*, 117.
39. *Institutes* II.8.46.
40. *Letters of John Calvin*, 4:375.
41. Wallace, *Calvin's Doctrine of the Word and Sacrament*, 120.
42. *Commentary on the Book of the Prophet Isaiah*, 52.
43. *Commentaries on the First Epistle to Timothy*, 114.

teaching."[44] The critical necessity of this duty is reflected in his declaration: "No one will ever be a good pastor, unless he shews himself to be a *father* to the Church that is committed to him."[45] Calvin was even willing to say, "The most important duty of the minister of the word is, to comfort wretched men, who are oppressed by afflictions, or who bend under their weight, and, in short, to point out what is true rest and serenity of mind."[46]

The example Calvin set presented a stark contrast to the masses of ignorant bishops and priests of his time.[47] Calvin himself made numerous polemical statements regarding the ministry of the Roman Catholic Church. He had a number of choice epithets which he directed at the papacy. The popes, in his judgment, were nothing but "swine and dogs."[48] The problem, he stated, was that "the Pope and his attendant train are wanting not merely in fidelity in the discharge of the office, but also in the ministry itself."[49] Why did the papacy have no ministry? The fundamental reason, Calvin charged, was that they "disdainfully throw away from themselves the office of teaching."[50]

The inferior clergy aligned with the papacy were no better. Calvin identified them as the Pope's "filthy clergy."[51] While the

44. *Institutes* III.4.12.

45. *Commentary on the First Epistle to the Thessalonians*, 254.

46. *Commentary on the Book of the Prophet Isaiah*, 53. The pastoral compassion that Calvin evidenced is discussed in a number of scholarly studies. See Grin, "Calvin Pasteur," 203; Stauffer, *L'Humanitéde Calvin*, 58–60; Wallace, *Calvin, Geneva and the Reformation*, 183.

47. Milner, *Calvin's Doctrine of the Church*, 134–38.

48. *Commentaries on the Book of the Prophet Jeremiah and the Lamentations*, 45.

49. *Commentary on the First Epistle of Paul to the Corinthians*, 151.

50. *Commentary on a Harmony of the Evangelists*, 383.

51. *Commentaries on the Book of the Prophet Jeremiah and the Lamentations*, 45.

bishops "make their appearance in a theatrical dress," "a horned mitre, a ring richly set in jewels, or a silver cross, and other trifles," they "banish from themselves the ministry of teaching."[52] The bishops, he contended, were for the most part "ignorant of all doctrine"[53] and "do not so much as once meddle with the function of teaching."[54] The ministry offered by the priests, he charged, was not any better: "In promoting priests . . . we see how the ignorant, and those utterly devoid of learning and prudence, are inducted without discrimination. Even in hiring a mule-driver, more regard is paid to his past life than in choosing a priest."[55]

Calvin did more than just provide a model of what a Reformed pastor ought to be—a bishop of souls rather than a temporal prince, a minister of the church rather than a magistrate of the state. He also established a suitable ministry for the Geneva church. This indeed was a major element in his reform program. When Calvin arrived in Geneva, he came to the conclusion that most of the pastors were rude, ignorant, and untrustworthy.[56] He immediately took steps to upgrade the quality of Geneva's ministry.[57] The church constitution he wrote stipulated that a man must not only be called by God but must also endure an intense examination by the Company of Pastors. The men who were approved by this body were judged to be sound in doctrine, able to teach, and blameless in conduct.[58]

52. *Commentaries on the First Epistle to Timothy*, 80.
53. *Commentaries on the Epistle to Titus*, 296–97.
54. *Commentary upon the Acts of the Apostles*, 256.
55. *The Necessity of Reforming the Church*, 204.
56. For a discussion on the clergy in Geneva before the Reformation, see Cahier-Buccelli, "Dans l'ombre de la Réforme," 367–89.
57. Chadwick, *The Reformation*, 83.
58. Reid, "John Calvin, Pastoral Theologian," 72, discusses the impact

THE DISTRIBUTION OF CHURCH AUTHORITY

The problematic nature of the construal that Calvin espoused a theocratic form of civil government has been demonstrated. The additional error that Calvin maintained an autocracy in church government is manifested by considering the consistory itself.[59] The government Calvin crafted for the church in Geneva deliberately distributed authority. Power was not held by a single individual. It was located rather in an ecclesiastical assembly composed of ministers and elders.[60] The additional fact that Calvin desired "fit" ministers and "fit" elders to sit on the consistory—gifted and capable men—shows that he wanted men who formed independent judgments, not individuals who meekly followed Calvin's dictates.[61]

With respect to the pastors who would join Calvin on the consistory, their suitability included the necessity of an inward sense of God's call to the pastoral office.[62] This sense of the divine summons, however, did not automatically open the door into the pastorate. The aspiring pastoral candidate was required

---

of Calvin's perspective regarding the pastor and scholar and teacher.

59. McKee, "The Offices of Elders and Deacons in the Classical Reformed Tradition," 347, states, "Objecting to any monarchical or clerical monopoly, Calvin insisted on leadership by a group, some of whom must be laity."

60. Kingdon, "Calvin's Socio-Political Legacy," 113, comments on the two constitutions Calvin penned in Geneva, the church constitution of 1541 and the Geneva state constitution of 1543: "Both of these constitutions display a strong preference for collective government. Neither of them incorporates any trace of the preference for monarchic or one-man government that most thinkers of the sixteenth century preferred."

61. McKee, "Calvin and His Colleagues as Pastors," 9–42.

62. *Ecclesiastical Ordinances*, 36.

to endure an intense examination of his doctrine and conduct by the Company of Pastors in order to discern his "fitness." The first part of the exam was intended to ascertain "whether he who is to be ordained has a good and sound knowledge of Scripture." The testing process was also designed to determine whether or not the candidate was gifted in communication, "to ascertain whether he is fit to teach." At this point the candidate was required to give an exposition of Scripture. The candidate for the ministry had to be a gifted man, but also blameless in his life.[63]

Calvin's stress upon a highly competent ministry helps to explain the phenomenon of an almost entirely foreign ministry in Geneva.[64] The likely explanation for this is that a foreign ministry was necessary to meet the high educational standards for a Geneva pastor. "All were expected to have advanced training, at the university level, if possible, including instruction in Greek and Hebrew."[65] The caliber of pastors who became the colleagues of Calvin in Geneva—outstanding men like Pierre Viret, Theodore Beza, Michael Cop, and others—shows that he had no desire to be "the big man" in Geneva.[66]

It must also be kept in mind that church power was by no means concentrated in the Company of Pastors, a clerical body. Calvin distributed ecclesiastical authority further by means of his commitment to the office of lay elder. For this office, Calvin wanted men who were religious, moral, and capable of exercising rule. The elected elders had to be "good living and honorable

---

63. Ibid.

64. The one exception was Jacques Bernard, who was a Genevan. Naphy, "Church and State in Calvin's Geneva," 16.

65. Kingdon, "Calvin and the Establishment of Consistory Discipline in Geneva," 164.

66. It should also be remembered that Calvin attempted to recruit Peter Martyr Vermigli to help in the work of teaching in Geneva.

men, without reproach and beyond all suspicion, above all who fear God and possess the gift of spiritual prudence."[67]

It is clear that Calvin was looking for a certain kind of man for this office—someone who knew how to govern, how to exercise authority over others. This is precisely what he was able to achieve. Each elder on the consistory was one of the civil magistrates who governed the city-state of Geneva.[68] Each of the lay elders who served on the consistory sat on one of the three councils that ruled the Geneva Republic.[69] The benefit of this arrangement was obvious: the governors of the church would be men with a proven ability to govern the state.

CHECKS UPON MINISTERIAL POWER

We have seen that the constitutional arrangement of the church in Geneva—which came from the pen of Calvin himself—provided for a system which was structured against theocratic and autocratic possibilities. Calvin distinguished between two spheres, the civil and the ecclesiastical. Within the ecclesiastical sphere, he distributed power between pastors and elders. There is, however, another point that should be made regarding the power that Calvin and his fellow pastors exercised. Their authority was limited not only by the principle of distribution, but also by the establishment of a significant check upon their conduct—the possibility of ministerial discipline for misbehavior.

---

67. *Ecclesiastical Ordinances*, 41–42.

68. Naphy, *Calvin and the Consolidation of the Genevan Reformation*, 77–78.

69. The *Ecclesiastical Ordinances*, 41, put it this way: "As this church is now placed, it will be desirable to elect two men from the Little Council, four from the Council of Sixty, and six from the Council of Two Hundred."

The problem with the construal of Calvin as a theocratic despot is that it does not seriously take into account the strong emphasis in the church constitution that all the pastors in Geneva—including Calvin himself—were accountable to church government. The principle of submission to church authority began from the moment that a man sought the pastoral office. The pastoral candidate had to submit to an examination of his doctrine and life by the Company of Pastors. He also had to submit himself to the established confessional perspective of the Geneva church.[70] The principle of accountability and submission to his brethren in the ministry continued after a ministerial candidate had been installed into office. There was the practical requirement that all the ministers of the Geneva church were obligated to attend a weekly meeting to discuss biblical doctrine. The obligatory nature of this meeting was reflected in the constitutional provision that "any man who is negligent over this is to be reprimanded."[71]

All the ministers in Geneva were subject not only to the Company of Pastors, but also to the Geneva Consistory. This body included all the pastors and the lay elders. The number of men who sat on the consistory varied from the moment it began to function in 1542 until the year of Calvin's death in 1564. In its first year of operation, there were nine pastors on the consistory; a generation later, in 1564, the number had increased to nineteen. During the same period, the number of lay elders remained fairly constant at twelve.[72] It was the full consistory,

---

70. *Ecclesiastical Ordinances*, 37.

71. Ibid. Even those pastors who ministered in the hinterland surrounding the walled city of Geneva were required to attend the weekly gathering for theological discussion.

72. Monter, "The Consistory of Geneva," 469. Cf. Kingdon, "Calvin and the Family," 5–6.

numbering between twenty and thirty men, that was given the responsibility of maintaining discipline over all the ministers.

Each pastor who desired to serve the Geneva church would understand quite well that no minister was "above the law." There would be no autocracy in the church. The determination of the church constitution regarding ministerial accountability and submission to the consistory government was clear: "Discipline will be imposed on him who merits it."[73]

The kind of discipline that would be imposed would depend upon the nature of the crime or vice. Calvin distinguished in the church constitution between two broad categories of possible ministerial sins. There were eighteen offences that fell into the category of the impermissible, "crimes which are altogether intolerable in a minister." There were also sixteen vices that were regarded as serious but not as problematic. These were "faults which may be endured provided that a fraternal admonition is offered."[74] On the basis of these broad categories of ministerial offenses, jurisdiction would be assigned in a specific case.

Calvin here manifested his legal mind, which had been developed first at Orléans under the French jurist Pierre de l'Estoile and then at Bourges under the tutelage of the Italian Andrea Alciato.[75] Calvin set forth three basic possibilities with respect to ministerial misbehavior. He envisioned the possibility that a pastor might commit a civil offense. He might fall into a sin that ought never to be found in a minister. Or he might plague the church by intolerable vices. With respect to each situation Calvin set forth the disciplinary procedure that needed to be followed.

73. *Ecclesiastical Ordinances*, 38.
74. Ibid.
75. Reid, "John Calvin, Lawyer and Legal Reformer," 150–53, provides a nice treatment of his legal training.

While ministerial vices could be handled by a "simple admonition,"[76] a civil offense would bring the case to the civil magistrates. The case would come before the Small Council, which stood at the apex of the hierarchy of the three councils that governed Geneva. It was composed of twenty-five citizens who wielded the real power in the Republic of Geneva.[77] What would the Small Council do to a pastor who had committed a crime? The church constitution declares, "The Seigneury shall take the matter in hand and, over and above the ordinary punishment customarily imposed on others, shall punish him by deposing him from office."[78] A serious ministerial sin entailed a dual jurisdiction. The case would first appear before the consistory, and then it would go to the civil court, the Small Council. Although the consistory had the right to discipline the minister, the constitution insists that "the final judgment concerning the punishment shall always be reserved to the Seigneury."[79] Thus, the Small Council had the final say, even in a case where there was a dual jurisdiction, the ecclesiastical and the civil. Republican principles would prevail. There would be no movement toward theocracy. The civil magistrates would have the final word rather than the clergy, even when a disciplinary case entailed one of their own.

The preceding discussion has demonstrated that Calvin in his political doctrine did not espouse a theocratic government, in which the ministers of the church exercised direct political authority. In the judgment of Calvin, the best form of government

---

76. *Ecclesiastical Ordinances*, 39.

77. As Höpfl, in *The Christian Polity of John Calvin*, 132, states, the Small Council had the ultimate authority in Geneva, "the power of life and death."

78. *Ecclesiastical Ordinances*, 39.

79. Ibid.

was the mixed government of a republic, composed of elected officials—the aristocracy—and enfranchised citizens with the right to democratic processes. He wrote, "I will not deny that aristocracy, or a system compounded of aristocracy and democracy, far excels all others."[80] The advantage of a republic, "where freedom is regulated with becoming moderation," related to the issue of liberty.[81] It is clear from his biblical commentary on Micah 5:5 that he believed the right to vote is a major constituent in what freedom actually entails: "In this especially consists the best condition of the people, when they can choose, by common consent, their own shepherds."[82] Nothing can be clearer than this; Calvin taught that the best condition for citizens was to live in a republic, to be under the civil authority of the very leaders the people themselves had chosen to political office.

It cannot be disputed, though, that the pastors of the Reformed church in Geneva had enormous influence in the Republic.[83] The consistory was "the effective motor behind the establishment of the first 'Puritan' society."[84] Pre-Reformation Geneva was a society characterized by moral laxity and debauchery, legal prostitution, illegitimate children, drunkenness, and gambling.[85] Post-Reformation Genevan society presented a striking contrast to this lax state of affairs.[86] Calvin longed for

---

80. *Institutes* IV.20.8.

81. Ibid.

82. *Commentaries on the Prophet Micah*, 309–10.

83. Kingdon, "Calvin and the Government of Geneva," 61–63.

84. Monter, "The Consistory of Geneva," 467.

85. Kingdon, "Calvin and the Establishment of Consistory Discipline in Geneva," 167; Kingdon, "The Control of Morals in Calvin's Geneva," 4.

86. Chadwick, *The Reformation*, 86.

the renovation of society by the power of the gospel.[87] What he looked for was actually achieved, "not simply the salvation of souls, but a Geneva that was reformed by the Word of God."[88] As the Scottish Reformer John Knox put it, "In other places, I confess Chryst to be trewlie preachit; but maneris and religion so sinceirlie reformat, I have not yit sene in any uther place."[89]

The moral influence of the Geneva pastors was enormous. Social renewal was the outcome. Indirect power, however, must not be confused with a theocratic government.[90] What was true of Calvin was true of all the pastors in the Geneva church, their power was "indirect and depended upon persuasion rather than upon political office or personal tyranny." Indeed, "it is a mistake to refer to this period as one of theocratic rule."[91]

---

87. Niebuhr, *Christ and Culture*, 217.

88. Leith, *Introduction to the Reformed Tradition*, 76. Cf., Schreiner, *The Theater of His Glory*, 107; Biáler, *L'umanesimo Sociale di Calvin*, 25.

89. Knox, *The Works of John Knox*, 4:240.

90. In the time of Calvin, theocratic government was to be found in the Jewish ghettos of Europe. Pfeffer, *Church, State, and Freedom*, 8, states, "The Jewish state almost to the contemporary era was the ghetto; its head was the rabbi; its constitution the Bible of Moses (Torah), and its laws, the Talmud and later rabbinic commentaries."

91. Spitz, *The Protestant Reformation*, 221.

2

The Making of War

HOLY WAR advocates throughout history believed that the church had the authority to declare war. In terms of the Crusades, it was a war authorized by the Pope. The First Crusade had been proclaimed by Pope Urban II in 1095 to liberate Jerusalem from Muslim control and oppression. The crusade mentality continued into the sixteenth century. A crusade league—including Spain, Venice, and the Papacy—defeated the Turks in the Battle of Lepanto on October 7, 1571.

While holy war doctrine in terms of the justice of war found a home within the Roman Catholic Church, what place, if any, did it have within the teaching of John Calvin? The allegation has been made that Calvin falls within the holy war camp, the tradition of the medieval crusade.[1] Did Calvin and the Reformed—or Luther, for that matter—believe that the church has the power to authorize war against foreign governments? Let us first consider the approach of Luther and then the teaching of Calvin, along with the doctrine espoused in Zurich.

Martin Luther spoke strongly against the medieval holy war tradition in his treatise *On War against the Turk*. "The pope and the bishops," he said, "would be destroying their calling and office to fight with the sword against flesh and blood." To do

---

1. Bainton, *Christian Attitudes toward War and Peace*, 144–45; George, "War and Peace in the Puritan Tradition," 494.

such a thing was "forbidden."[2] He focused upon the head of the Catholic Church: "It is not right for the pope ... to lead a church army."[3] He even denounced two popes, Julius and Clement,[4] as he expressed his dissatisfaction with the crusade ideology, in which "the pope, along with his followers, wages war."[5]

Even as Luther firmly rejected medieval holy war doctrine, he insisted that the civil magistrate alone is authorized to make war. In his piece *Against the Robbing and Murdering Hordes of Peasants*, he stated, "A prince and lord must remember that according to Romans 13 he is God's minister and a servant of his wrath and that the sword has been given to him to use."[6] With reference to the Turkish threat against Germany, it was the duty of the "Emperor, the kings, and princes" to "protect their subjects."[7] Luther even went so far as to chastise the Emperor for his inactivity pertaining to the threat posed by Suleyman and his Turkish horde. "It is not difficult to show," he complained, "that up to now the banner has been regarded as a mere piece of silk, for otherwise the emperor would long ago have unfurled it, the princes would have followed it, and the Turk would not have become so mighty."[8]

While Luther belabored the point that the secular magistrate alone—not the pope or the church—had the authority to initiate war, Calvin restricted the right to make war to the civil magistrate largely in opposition to the idea of a private individual doing so. This careful differentiation appears in the *Institutes*,

2. *On War against the Turk*, 165.
3. Ibid., 168.
4. Ibid., 169.
5. Ibid., 180.
6. *Against the Robbing and Murdering Hordes of Peasants*, 52–53.
7. *On War against the Turk*, 187.
8. Ibid., 190.

the biblical commentaries, and in the sermons.[9] Let us begin by noting this distinction between the command of God for public vengeance and the prohibition against private vengeance as it appears in his *locus* on war in *Institutes* IV.20.10–12.[10]

Before Calvin moved to discuss war per se, he first dealt with the civil magistrate and his responsibility to exercise public vengeance against domestic evil. Whereas the private Christian is forbidden to kill, it is a much different thing for the magis-

---

9. The importance of studying "Calvin's sermons with a view to the understanding of his theological and exegetical ideals" is reflected upon by Armstrong, "Exegetical and Theological Principles in Calvin's Preaching," 191. Armstrong reminds us that "the largest part of Calvin's work in Geneva was unquestionably dedicated to his preaching, an activity which produced . . . some 4,000+ sermons."

10. Paragraphs 10 through 12 appear in the final chapter of Book IV. Chapter 20 addresses the subject of the civil magistrate. The term *locus* as Calvin used it can refer to an entire chapter. In *Institutes* IV.20.1, the word *locus* is used to refer to the entirety of the twentieth chapter, which is a *locus* on the broad topic of civil government. At other times the word *locus* refers to a subsection of a chapter. An example of this is found in *Institutes* IV.20.3. Here, in the midst of his *locus* on civil government, Calvin stated in the first sentence that there would be a more appropriate *locus* to speak about the practice of civil government. The point to take note of is simply this: Calvin regarded all thirty-two paragraphs in Chapter 20 as constituting a *locus*; but he also viewed one subdivision of this larger *locus*—the topic of the practice of civil government—as being a *locus*. It appears that he began this *locus* on the practice of civil government in *Institutes* IV.20.9, focusing upon this more narrow topic from IV.20.9 to IV.20.13. It was within this more narrow *locus* on the practice of civil government that Calvin presented his just war doctrine in IV.20.10–12. The Latin text of these passages may be examined as it appears in *Ioannis Calvini Opera*, vol. 2. See col. 1092 and col. 1094.

trates.[11] Calvin identified them as the "vicars of God"[12] who had a sword put into their hand by God himself "to be drawn against all murderers."[13] As the vicar of God, the magistrate carried out "the very judgments of God." Calvin urged "princes and other rulers" to "apply themselves to this ministry."[14]

Having dealt with the subject of public vengeance with respect to the murderer in *Institutes* IV.20.10, Calvin transitioned to the related matter of public vengeance upon an invading army in the next paragraph. In his argument he reasoned from the lesser to the greater: "Indeed, if they rightly punish those robbers whose harmful acts have affected only a few, will they allow a whole country to be afflicted and devastated by robbers with impunity?"[15] The answer Calvin expected is obvious. No prince would allow such a thing to happen to his country. For Calvin, "both natural equity and the nature of the office dictate that princes must be armed . . . to defend by war the dominions entrusted to their safekeeping."[16] The private individual does not have such authority. "It is not for everyone to take the sword in hand," he

---

11. *Institutes* IV.20.11. The same distinction appears in his biblical commentaries. In his *Commentaries on the Last Four Books of Moses*, 52–53, Calvin wrote against private revenge, arguing that it was not lawful for "a private person to assume the sword." On the other hand, he contended in his *Commentary on a Harmony of the Evangelists*, 297, "God had enjoined, by his law that judges and magistrates should punish those who had done injuries, by making them endure as much as they had inflicted." His public preaching sounded the same theme. In Sermon 118 of his *Sermons on Deuteronomy*, 724, he noted that the Christian endures, while the magistrate resists.

12. *Institutes* IV.20.6.

13. *Institutes* IV.20.10.

14. Ibid.

15. *Institutes* IV.20.11.

16. Ibid.

declared in Sermon 30 in his preaching through 2 Samuel. "The authority of our princes must, therefore, guide us." The war had to be "undertaken by a just authority," he said. If that were the case, we may conclude that "it is good and legitimate."[17]

THE AUGUSTINIAN FOUNDATION

For Calvin, the issue of the proper authority was an indispensable element in the just war. He, in fact, began his treatment of just war doctrine in the same way that Thomas Aquinas had in his *Summa Theologica*. In his famous essay *De bello*,[18] Aquinas stated, "In order for a war to be just, three things are necessary." He then mentioned the first of three necessary constituents that must be included in a war that is just: "First, the authority of the sovereign by whose command the war is to be waged. For it is not the business of a private individual to declare war, because he can seek for redress of his rights from the tribunal of his superior. Moreover it is not the business of a private individual to summon together the people, which has to be done in wartime."[19]

As we shall note later in this study, Calvin likewise included Aquinas' other two constituents of the just war—a just cause and a right intention.[20] It should here be appreciated that

17. *Sermons on 2 Samuel*, 459.

18. Aquinas' influential treatment of just war doctrine is presented in *Summa Theologica* 2a2ae, q. 40, art. 1–4. In Question 40, Aquinas considered four fundamental questions: *First.* Are some wars permissible? *Second.* May clerics engage in war? *Third.* May belligerents use deception, such as an ambush? *Fourth.* May war be conducted on holy days?

19. *Summa Theologica* 2a2ae, q. 40, art. 1. All quotations from Aquinas' essay *Of War* are from the five-volume English translation *Summa Theologica*.

20. The just cause looks to the past—something must have already happened that justifies going to war. The right intention looks to the future; it focuses attention upon what the government intends to achieve

Aquinas' discussion in the thirteenth century was nothing new. The same three elements of a just war were found in the teaching of Augustine of Hippo. It seems quite clear that Aquinas moved the discussion back to the patristic framework after other medieval doctors had developed more complex discussions of what a just war actually is. Alexander of Hales, for example, required six constituents for a war to be just in his *Summa Theologiae*: there had to be the proper authority, attitude, intention, condition, merit, and cause.[21] Aquinas simply returned the just war formula back to the original rather simple definition initially proposed by Augustine.[22]

In Augustine's classic treatment of just war doctrine, he wrote that there was "no need here to enter on the long discussion of just and unjust wars."[23] He merely affirmed in this statement that he would not enter into a *long* discussion on this topic, but he would in fact say *something* about it. The justice or injustice of a particular war, he affirmed, depends on certain factors, which he then went on to develop. In one sentence, he specified the three constituents that Aquinas would later include as being the three necessary things for a war to be just. Augustine put it this way: "A great deal depends on the causes for which men undertake wars, and on the authority they have for doing so; for the natural order which seeks the peace of mankind, ordains that the monarch should have the power of undertaking war if he thinks it advisable, and that the soldiers should perform their military duties in behalf of the peace and safety of the community."[24]

---

by going to war.

21. Russell, *The Just War in the Middle Ages*, 220.
22. Ibid., 269.
23. *Reply to Faustus the Manichaean* XXII.74.
24. *Reply to Faustus the Manichaean* XXII.75. The Latin text of this

Here Augustine presented the crucial elements to which Aquinas would later appeal. While Aquinas would mention the authority of the sovereign, Augustine spoke about how the natural order ordained that the monarch had the authority to make war. While Aquinas discussed the necessity of a just cause, Augustine referred to the importance of the causes for which wars were undertaken.[25] While Aquinas stressed that there had to be a rightful intention, Augustine wrote about seeking the peace of mankind and prosecuting a war in behalf of peace.

In his discussion of the just war in the *Institutes*, Calvin explicitly connected his teaching with Augustine by referring to him two times by name.[26] He thereby deliberately positioned himself in the mainstream of the just war tradition of the church. There is no doubt that Calvin had a profound admiration for the bishop of Hippo.[27] There is some legitimacy to the conception that with respect to his own theology, Calvin borrowed from Augustine "with both hands."[28] Although Calvin recognized

---

passage may be examined in *Contra Faustum Manichaeum*.

25. In the teaching of Augustine, the constituent of a just cause with respect to the justice of a war is closely tied in with the element of the proper authority that is necessary to start a war. See the discussion provided by Deane, *The Political and Social Ideas of St. Augustine*, 162.

26. *Institutes* IV.20.12.

27. Singer, *John Calvin*, 7.

28. Wendel, *Calvin*, 124. We should not think, however, that Calvin concurred with the totality of Augustine's teachings. In his biblical commentary upon 1 Corinthians 3:15, Calvin provided an illuminating statement that shows how he regarded Augustine and several other theologians of the church. In his *Commentary on the First Epistle of Paul to the Corinthians*, 140, Calvin declared, "It is certain that Paul speaks of those who, while always retaining the *foundation*, mix *hay* with *gold*, *stubble* with *silver*, and *wood* with *precious stones*—that is, who build upon Christ, but in consequence of the weakness of the flesh, admit something that is man's, or through ignorance turn aside to some extent from the

that Augustine did not provide an infallible interpretation of the biblical text at every point, he did believe that Augustine's doctrine of the just war faithfully reflected the word of God.

Although Calvin did not explicitly connect his teaching on the just war with Aquinas, it could well be the case that he had read his treatment *De bello* in *Summa Theologica*. We know for a fact that Calvin read Aquinas either directly or by means of intermediate sources.[29] He mentioned Aquinas by name in the *Institutes*.[30] Many writers in the sixteenth century, Catholic and Protestant, looked to Aquinas for insight on this issue.[31] Perhaps Calvin was included in this group of writers who carefully weighed what the great Dominican had to say about war. We can definitely conclude that the teaching of Calvin on the just war stood firmly in the Augustinian tradition and its trajectory, which Aquinas picked up in the thirteenth century.[32]

THOMISM IN ZURICH

There is stronger evidence that Calvin's contemporaries—the Zurich theologians, Henry Bullinger and Peter Martyr Vermigli—carefully examined what Aquinas expounded on the doctrine of the just war. Let us briefly consider the imprint of Aquinas' thinking upon their teaching.

---

strict purity of God's word. Such were many of the saints, Cyprian, Ambrose, Augustine, and the like."

29. Lane, *John Calvin*, 45. Cf. Wendel, *Calvin*, 126–27.

30. *Institutes* II.11.4 and III.22.9.

31. Johnson, *Just War Tradition and the Restraint of War*, xxv.

32. Vos, *Aquinas, Calvin, and Contemporary Protestant Thought*, 161, argues that "on several points of major importance" there are "striking parallels between" Aquinas and Calvin. This present study demonstrates that there are indeed fundamental parallels between the two theologians on the doctrine of the just war.

Bullinger dealt with this doctrine in the context of a lengthy discussion on the civil magistrate in Sermons 6–9 of the *Decades*.[33] His scholastic methodology is evident in his treatment. A scholastic order of teaching traditionally addresses three questions: Does it exist? (*An sit?*) What is it? (*Quid sit?*) Of what sort is it? (*Quia sit?*). Bullinger began by addressing these questions.

Magistrates, in the first place, do exist, and they are described by various terms: power, authority, domination, princes, consuls, and kings.[34] The magistracy, in the second place, he contended, is an office that should be biblically defined. Referring to the origin of the office, the end in view, and the way in which the end is to be achieved, Bullinger explained what the magistracy is in these terms: "The magistracy, by the scriptures, may be defined to be a divine ordinance or action, whereby the good being defended by the prince's aid, and the evil suppressed by the same authority, godliness, justice, honesty, peace and tranquility, both public and private, are safely preserved."[35] He

---

33. Sermons 6–9 on the civil magistrate appear in the second decade of the five decades that constitute Bullinger's *Decades*. The collected edition of the *Decades* was first published in 1552. The 1587 English translation published in London by Ralph Newberrie was entitled *Fifty Godlie and Learned Sermons, Divided into Five Decades Containing the Chiefe and Principall Points of Christian Religion*. Parker, *Calvin's Preaching*, 17, describes it as a "coherent practical theology, if not an actual dogmatics." Muller, *Christ and the Decree*, 39, makes the point that it covers the full spectrum of Christian theology. Dowey, "Heinrich Bullinger As Theologian," 52–53, suggests that the sermons, which were delivered in Latin rather than in the German vernacular, were probably preached to the city pastors and teachers of the city at the Zurich *Prophezei*. Opitz, "Bullinger's *Decades*," 104, agrees that this may have been the case, although he concedes that it is not completely clear as to whether or not Bullinger actually preached all fifty sermons of the *Decades*.

34. Sermon 6, *Decades*, 309.

35. Ibid. The Latin text of this definition may be examined in

explained in the third place that there are three different sorts of magistracies—*monarchia, aristocratia,* and *democratia.*[36]

Bullinger clearly reflected the style of scholastic methodology.[37] Is there evidence that he studied and embraced Aquinas' teaching in *De bello* pertaining to the matter of the *justice of war*? With respect to the category of *justice in war*, Bullinger indeed opened the door to holy war practice. This we shall see in the next chapter. When it comes to the matter of *jus ad bellum*, however, he seems to bear the impress of Aquinas. Even before he treated the doctrine of war at length in Sermon 9, he briefly presented his understanding of what constituted the just war in Sermon 6. In one paragraph, he presented in order the three Thomistic elements of the just war. Bullinger insisted first upon the proper authority, the civil magistrate. He said, secondly, that there had to be a just cause. He maintained, thirdly, that there had to be a right intention, the confirmation of peace.[38]

Peter Martyr Vermigli, perhaps even more than Bullinger, reflected in his essay *De bello* the methodological style of medieval scholastic theology—and probably a deliberate attempt to reproduce the actual substance of Aquinas' teaching on the just war.[39]

Sermonum Decades Quinque, 150.

36. Sermon 6, *Decades*, 309–10.

37. Bullinger's treatment of the civil magistrate also mirrors the disputational form of argumentation that was used in formal academic theology in the medieval universities. In fact, Bullinger and Vermigli (and Calvin, to some extent, in the *Institutes*) will often proceed in the development of a doctrine by presenting an *objectio* followed by a *responsio*. Beza, as we shall see, follows the same scholastic procedure in his treatise *Du droit des magistrats*.

38. Sermon 6, *Decades*, 307–8.

39. Muller, *Christ and the Decree*, 72, makes the statement that "the chief importance of his systematic essays was their Thomistic method."

His theological excursus on war originally appeared at the end of his biblical commentary on 2 Samuel 2.[40] The structure of his commentaries was to include theological *loci* at strategic places in the midst of his running commentary on the biblical text.[41] While Calvin incorporated doctrinal topics in his *Institutes*, Vermigli left them embedded in his commentaries.[42] After Vermigli died, the doctrinal *loci* that were scattered throughout his biblical commentaries were abstracted from their original setting, gathered together, and arranged in a format resembling Calvin's *Institutes*.[43] The essay *De bello* was removed from its place at the end of his exposition on 2 Samuel 2, and it was placed in the fourth part of what became *The Common Places*. The *locus* on war is presented in Chapter 17, and it consists of thirty-three sections.

With respect to the topic of war, Vermigli's *De bello* from the outset seems to be providing answers to the three traditional questions that the medieval mind would ask concerning any subject of discussion. With respect to the topic of war, Vermigli from the outset seems to be providing answers to the three traditional questions that the medieval mind would ask concerning any subject of discussion.

As to the first question—Does it exist?—Vermigli seems to have been answering it by way of the opening statement in

40. Kingdon, "The Political Thought of Peter Martyr Vermigli," 123.

41. The approach of Vermigli was different than that taken by Calvin, with his commitment to *brevitas et facilitas* in his writing of biblical commentaries.

42. Thompson, "The Survival of Allegorical Argumentation in Peter Martyr Vermigli's Old Testament Exegesis," 256, makes the point that "such a format grew out of a widespread and considered view that Christian doctrines ought to emerge from the soil of Scripture itself."

43. Kingdon, "Peter Martyr Vermigli and the Marks of the True Church," 203–4.

the *locus*: "Because in the holie Historie, there is often mention made of war: I thought good to speake somewhat of that matter."[44] He was making the simple point that wars do exist. The second question raised by the medieval student—What is it?—was likewise answered in the opening section: "And just warre maie thus not unaptly be defined. It is an Hostile dissention whereby through the Princes edict mischiefes are repressed by force and Armes, to the intent that men may peaceably and quietly live by justice and godlinesse."[45] The answer to the third question—Of what sort is it?—was likewise addressed in due order: "Hereof are gathered those three properties which commonly are ascribed unto right warfaring. First, that there is required the authoritie of the Prince: Secondly, an honest cause, to wit, that peace be sought for: Lastly that it be done with a good mind."[46]

For Vermigli to proceed in such a way as this, providing the answers to the customary questions that were raised in a scholarly setting, seems to be almost a reflexive action, a result of his years of training in scholastic theology at the University of Padua.[47]

Vermigli did not quote Aquinas by name in his *locus* on war, though the essay is replete with explicit references to Augustine. Nevertheless, his theological essays reflected a style that was reminiscent of Aquinas, and it also seems fairly clear

---

44. *Of Warre or Battell*, in *The Political Thought of Peter Martyr Vermigli*, 61. The *locus* provided by Kingdon in this volume presents paragraphs 1 through 20 of Vermigli's full *locus* of 33 paragraphs in *The Common Places*. All future citations will be from the 1583 London publication.

45. *The Common Places* IV.17.1.

46. *The Common Places* IV.17.2.

47. Donnelly, "Calvinist Thomism," 442–43; Kingdon, "The Function of Law in the Political Thought of Peter Martyr Vermigli," 166; McNair, *Peter Martyr in Italy*, 116–17.

that the substance of Vermigli's just war doctrine—pertaining to the category of the *jus ad bellum*—was heavily informed by Aquinas.

Two pieces of evidence suggest that Vermigli framed his discussion on just war against the background of his teaching in Thomist doctrine. First, Aquinas was the medieval theologian who pared down the requirements for a just war to three things. Vermigli may well have been referring to this Thomistic conception in his statement that there are "three properties which commonly are ascribed unto right warfaring."[48] Secondly, his one-sentence definition of what a just war actually is seems to follow the very order of Aquinas' delineation of the three things that are necessary for a just war—the authority of the sovereign, a just cause (specifically, that there is some fault in those who are attacked), and a rightful intention (namely, the advancement of the good). Vermigli, once again, defined the just war in this way: "It is an hostile dissention whereby through the Princes edict mischiefes are repressed by force and Armes, to the intent that men may peaceably and quietly live by justice and godlinesse."[49]

The preceding discussion has demonstrated that neither Calvin nor the Reformed in Zurich embraced the holy war doctrine that the church had the authority to initiate armed conflict. The Reformed tradition, both in Geneva and Zurich, maintained the classic position of the just war tradition that the civil magistrate alone had the right given to him by God to declare and prosecute war when there was a just cause. Calvin, just like Augustine and Luther as well, believed that the first and indispensable constituent relative to the matter of the justice of war was that the civil government alone had the authority to begin a war. Although the papacy continued to embrace the

---

48. *The Common Places* IV.17.2.
49. *The Common Places* IV.17.1.

crusade ideology—that it is legitimate for a bishop, including the pope, to wage war—such a holy war perspective found no advocates within the Reformed community.

3

Godly Warfare

THE EMPHASIS in the medieval period was upon the *jus ad bellum*.[1] We must appreciate the fact, however, that the medieval writers were not oblivious to the distinction between the *justice of war* and *justice in war*.

> War is always judged twice, first with reference to the reasons states have for fighting, secondly with reference to the means they adopt. The first kind of judgment is adjectival in character: we say that a particular war is just or unjust. The second is adverbial: we say that the war is being fought justly or unjustly. Medieval writers made the difference a matter of prepositions, distinguishing *jus ad bellum*, the justice of war, from *jus in bello*, justice in war.[2]

At this point in our study of Calvin's teaching on the state and war, we turn our attention to his relationship to the medieval doctrine of the law of war, the *jus in bello*. The traditional restraints of the church's teaching had to do with the weapons of war that were allowable and with discriminating between combatants and noncombatants. The two main historical components of the *jus in bello* appear in terms of "two sets of legal or customary

---

1. Johnson, *Ideology, Reason, and the Limitation of War*, 39.
2. Walzer, *Just and Unjust Wars*, 21.

restraints: those of the extent of harm, if any, that might be done to noncombatants, and those on the weapons of war."[3]

With respect to the weapons of war, the Second Lateran Council in 1139 placed a ban on the employment of certain weapons in battles among Christians. The forbidden weapons included crossbows and siege machines (Canon 29).[4] Such weapons, however, were deemed to be legitimate in wars against Muslims and other heretics. The attempt by the medieval church to restrain war is also seen in the Peace of God movement in the thirteenth century under Pope Gregory IX. Eight kinds of people were specified in the treatise *Of Truces and Peace* as enjoying noncombatant immunity. "*De Treuga et Pace* lists eight classes of persons who should have full security against the ravages of war: clerics, monks, friars, other religious, pilgrims, travelers, merchants, and peasants cultivating the soil. The animals and goods of such persons were also protected, as well as the peasants' lands."[5]

How did Calvin relate to this medieval tradition—with its two customary restraints on weapons employed and harm administered? As we shall see, Calvin strongly emphasized the call of the medieval church for restraint in battle, teaching the necessity of humanity in war. In his repeated exhortations for restraint in battle, he manifested continuity with the Peace of God movement in the Middle Ages. At the same time, his doctrine differed from the theoretical reflections of Bullinger and Vermigli on the conduct of war and with the actual practice of the Ottoman Turks in the Balkans. On the matter of military arms, however, Calvin recognized the legitimacy of all the available weapons of his time, not adopting the medieval limits upon the crossbow or the siege machine.

3. Johnson, *Just War Tradition and the Restraint of War*, xxxiii.
4. Ibid., 128.
5. Ibid., 127.

THE WEAPONS OF WAR

The sixteenth century was a transitional period in terms of the kind of army that took the field. Battles were no longer like the classical medieval engagement between heavily armored knights on horseback. The modern army that emerged in the sixteenth century gave a more prominent place to the soldier on foot, although men on horseback did not entirely disappear. The foot soldiers of the time included pike men, who were invaluable in stopping the charge of heavy cavalry. There were also archers, and there were harquebusiers. It was the presence of the latter, bringing about the general use of arms by foot soldiers on the field of battle, that would especially characterize the modern army.[6]

In addition to the presence of thousands of foot soldiers armed with the harquebus, the sixteenth-century battlefield was transformed by the widespread use of the cannon, cared for and operated by the artillerymen.[7] The arrival of eight-foot-long bronze cannons in large number onto the field of battle, such as were used by the House of Valois beginning with King Charles VIII, obviously brought changes in strategy and tactics—in addition to providing the opportunity for increased casualties and terror.

What did Calvin think about such weaponry? It needs to be recognized that he was very much in tune with developments in his own time and in ancient history as well. He referred, for example, to the chariots used in the ancient world and how they had "great blades attached" that "could rout an army."[8] With reference to his own period of time, he spoke about artillery and the distinction between foot soldiers and cavalry.[9] In Calvin's

6. Rice and Grafton, *The Foundations of Early Modern Europe*, 12.
7. Johnson, *Just War Tradition and the Restraint of War*, 181.
8. Sermon 31, *Sermons on 2 Samuel*, 471.
9. Sermon 116, *Sermons on Deuteronomy*, 713; Sermon 117, *Sermons*

thinking, the art of war necessitated the use of any number of military provisions. The "right to wage war," he wrote, "furnishes the reason for garrisons, leagues, and other civil defenses." He defined "civil defenses" as "things used in the art of war."[10] Calvin clearly believed that since war is lawful, the constituent elements of war are lawful—namely, weapons and their use in the broader category of strategy and tactics.

The one tactic Calvin discussed was the ambush, a familiar topic of discussion for medieval theologians. Because of the deception involved in an ambush, some maintained that it was not just. The thinking was that since ambushes are a "kind of deception," they "seem to pertain to injustice." It would therefore be "unlawful to lay ambushes," even in a just war.[11] Aquinas did not believe that ambushes were morally problematic, and neither did Calvin. "If war, then, is lawful," Calvin maintained, "it is beyond all controversy that the usual methods of conquering may be lawfully employed, provided always that there be no violation of faith once pledged either by truce or in any other way."[12]

Wiles and deception, Calvin recognized, are at the very heart of making war. Like John of Salisbury, who had written that "he who hopes for favorable issues should fight by art and not by chance,"[13] Calvin pointed out that "the best commanders" are those "who accomplish more by art and counsel than by mere violence." Although tactical deception is legitimate, Calvin understood that every conceivable form of deception is not authorized in a time of war—there must be "no violation of faith

---

on Deuteronomy, 721.

10. *Institutes* IV.20.12.
11. *Summa Theologica* 2a2ae, q. 40, art. 3.
12. *Commentaries on the Book of Joshua*, 125.
13. Salisbury, *Policraticus* VI.20.

once pledged."[14] At this point he stood in line with the theological ethics of Aquinas. He had argued that "the plan of campaign"—which may include the tactic of an ambush—"ought" to be "hidden from the enemy." Conversely, "the breaking of a promise" is "always unlawful." Aquinas emphatically declared, "No one ought to deceive the enemy in this way, for there are certain *rights of war and covenants, which ought to be observed even among enemies.*"[15]

Calvin did not have continuity with the mindset manifested at the Second Lateran Council, which forbade crossbows and siege machines. Speaking about the rulers of the time, Calvin declared, "They have thus many footemen, thus many horsemen, thus much artillerie, such and such intelligence, such and such alyances." Here Calvin mentioned the weapon of choice for maximum firepower in the sixteenth century—artillery, the cannon. Did he suggest that such an overwhelming instrument of violence be banned from the field of battle? He did not. He rather affirmed, "True it is that all these things are necessarie for the warres."[16] In this perspective he stood with Luther, who acknowledged, "It is true that one should have horses and men and weapons and everything that is needed for battle, if they are to be had, so that one does not tempt God."[17]

The most powerful weapon of the time was the cannon. It was becoming a widespread instrument of havoc and destruction upon the battlefields of Europe. The possession of it seemed to guarantee victory. But like Vermigli, who stressed the importance of putting "confidence in God" rather than in

14. *Commentaries on the Book of Joshua*, 125.
15. *Summa Theologica* 2a2ae, q. 40, art. 3.
16. Sermon 117, *Sermons on Deuteronomy*, 721.
17. *On War against the Turk*, 191.

the possession of weapons,[18] Calvin warned that princes and armies must not place their trust in their weapons. This was the problem with the so-called Christian princes of his time, Calvin maintained. "We see all their trust is in their owne force and furniture," he complained.[19] The problem with such an attitude was that "the welfare of the Church consisteth neither in horses, nor in Chariotes, nor in Speares, nor in any manner of armour or artillerie; but in the power of God."[20]

Kings had a tendency to trust in one thing in particular, the war horse. It was a vice of the sixteenth century, and it was a fault of antiquity as well. Calvin drew attention to this in his exegesis of the divine command in Deuteronomy 17:16 that the king should not multiply horses for himself. "I have no doubt, then," he wrote, "that God condemns an immoderate number of horses from the consequences which might ensue." What, then, might result, if a king were to have a vast horde of horses and warriors capable of fighting upon them? Like Luther who warned that pride must be rooted out of the hearts of soldiers,[21] Calvin showed his deep-seated mistrust of human nature in terms of its propensity to fall into the sin of pride. He continued, "Thus, amongst other evils which might arise from a multitude of horses, Moses mentions this, that the king's mind will be puffed up with pride, so as to invade Egypt with an army of horse."[22]

The issue as to whether or not there was sin in the camp was a very serious thing. Calvin affirmed that defeat on the bat-

18. *The Common Places* IV.17.27.
19. Sermon 117, *Sermons on Deuteronomy*, 721.
20. Sermon 116, *Sermons on Deuteronomy*, 713.
21. *On War against the Turk*, 190.
22. *Commentaries on the Last Four Books of Moses*, 96. Cf., *Commentaries on the Book of Joshua*, 169.

tlefield was due to sin. This perspective was not unique to him. Bullinger had said the exact same thing. An army, he had contended, ought to be filled with a "chosen band of tried men."[23] The consequences of having something less than this were serious indeed. What was the fruit of fielding evil men, "a beastly drove of filthy swine"?[24] Bullinger answered, "The Turks overrun us and spoil us," and "we are to all the heathen a jesting-stock to laugh at."[25] The theme of a chosen band was likewise found in Calvin, but he particularly placed the stress upon the avoidance of the sin of unbelief. In his exposition of the command of God in Deuteronomy 20:1, which warned Israel not to be afraid when they went out to battle and saw vast armies arrayed before them with horses and chariots and soldiers, Calvin declared, "Now then if wee trust not to that which our Lord hath promised, then is it meete that hee should withdrawe himselfe from us and give us over."[26] In order to obtain the victory through the help of God, such men who were filled with unbelief and faintheartedness had to be removed from the army; "that rabble, which are good for nothing" had to be shaken off from the rest of the soldiers.[27]

As we have seen, Calvin did not show continuity with the approach of the Second Lateran Council, in which the church attempted to promote justice in war by limiting the kind of weapons that could be employed by Christian armies engaged in battle against one another. Calvin reasoned that since war is lawful, all the constituent elements of war, including the most advanced weapons of the time, must be legitimate. He only

23. Sermon 9, *Decades*, 381.
24. Ibid.
25. Ibid., 382.
26. Sermon 117, *Sermons on Deuteronomy*, 720.
27. Ibid.

warned that the Christian army must be wary of trusting in such military hardware and accoutrements rather than in the Living God. Calvin did, however, show continuity with the just war teaching of the church in its advocacy of humanity and restraint in battle.

THE WAGING OF WAR

Holy war differs from just war on this very matter of whether the war is prosecuted with humanity and restraint or not. In the just war there will be respect toward prisoners, the sparing of noncombatants, and the restraint of violence "within the limits of military necessity."[28] Holy war is just the opposite; "the war shall be prosecuted unsparingly."[29] It could be directed against any number of possible victims—combatants or noncombatants, seditious rebels or an invading army, infidels or even Christians.

There is no doubt that holy war teaching found a home in certain quarters among the seventeenth-century English Reformed and that it was much more than a speculative theory.[30]

28. Bainton, *Christian Attitudes toward War and Peace*, 249.

29. Ibid.

30. William Gouge (1575–1653) was the most eminent Puritan theologian who embraced holy war doctrine. He was a graduate of Cambridge University. He earned a doctorate in theology and was an excellent Hebraist. He wrote several theological treatises and a two-volume folio commentary on Hebrews. He served as a pastor in the parish of Black Friars in London for forty-five years, and he was a member of the Westminster Assembly. He set forth his doctrine of holy war in the third treatise of *Gods Three Arrowes*. He affirmed that "Papists profess the Christian Faith, yet are Anti-Christians, the directest and deadliest enemies that Christs true Church ever had" (213). This statement by itself does not distinguish Gouge from the classic just war doctrine of the Christian church. However, his declaration that "Papists are to Protestants as Amalekites to Israelites" was quite significant (188). The Israelites were commanded in Deuteronomy 25:17–19 to wage holy war

The Puritan armies in the English Civil War put holy war doctrine into practice. The Roundheads prosecuted the war effort against the Cavaliers and their supporters with ruthless abandon, eliminating not only men, but also women and children in their engagements.

The question that remains a matter of dispute relates to the source of Puritan thinking regarding the waging of war. In the wars of religion that followed the Reformation, Catholics and Protestants "inherited the doctrine of the holy war for the faith."[31] From whom did the Puritans inherit their doctrine of the holy war? Some scholars insist upon a connection between Calvin and later Puritan teaching. It is affirmed that Calvin falls within the holy war camp, the tradition of the medieval crusade.[32] According to other scholars, Bullinger was the source for holy war among the English Reformed.[33]

It is best that we bypass the question as to the actual source of Puritan holy war doctrine. Whether William Gouge, the renowned holy war advocate among the English Reformed, was influenced by Calvin or Bullinger is probably an unanswerable question. The narrow issue we shall consider relates to the actual trajectory of holy war doctrine among the Reformed. Is there a doctrinal trajectory from Calvin to Gouge or from Bullinger to Gouge? Were the holy war advocates among the English Reformed a continuation of the tradition established in Geneva or Zurich? We shall argue that it was the Zurich theologians, Bullinger and Vermigli, who planted the seeds of holy war doc-

---

and to exterminate the Amalekites. The implication for Protestant armies was obvious.

31. Johnson, *Just War Tradition and the Restraint of War*, 169.

32. Bainton, *Christian Attitudes toward War and Peace*, 144–45; George, "War and Peace in the Puritan Tradition," 494.

33. Johnson, *Ideology, Reason, and the Limitation of* War, 83; Klempa, "War and Peace in Puritan Thought," 88.

trine within the Reformed tradition.[34] Calvin could not have been the source for the holy war doctrine that many Puritans embraced, since he adamantly insisted upon humanity and restraint in war.

Although Calvin did discuss elements of Christian teaching on the justice of war in the *Institutes*,[35] he said next to nothing about justice in war, that the war must be fought justly. His teaching about godly warfare, the righteous way to fight, came in his commentaries and sermons.

As we examine Calvin's doctrine, we must keep in mind that his teaching regarding justice in war was developed against the backdrop of the advance of the Ottoman Turks, when the territorial integrity of the European heartland looked ominous for some time in the sixteenth century.[36] The inimical feelings Calvin had about Turkish warfare came to the surface when he declared, "Nowadayes the lawe of the Turk reigneth among Christians."[37] He was here referring to the Turkish commitment to total war and, more particularly, their tactic of burning—a feature that Bullinger also referred to in his reference to "the Mahometans" who "burne" and "hath so wasted the world with fire."[38] But the feature of Turkish warfare that distinguished it from the just war tradition that Calvin embraced was its disregard of justice in war. Ottoman disdain for the *jus in bello* practice of restraint in battle was reflected at Mohacs in 1526.

---

34. Although some scholars have correctly maintained that Bullinger taught holy war, no one has drawn attention to the fact that Vermigli likewise made a contribution to holy war doctrine among the Reformed.

35. *Institutes* IV.20.11–12.

36. Suleyman was unsuccessful in his attempt to take Vienna in 1529. He made another attempt in 1532 which likewise failed.

37. Sermon 119, *Sermons on Deuteronomy*, 734.

38. Sermon 41, *A Hundred Sermons upon the Apocalipse of Jesus Christ*, 125.

Suleyman's policy of taking no prisoners resulted in the annihilation of some 30,000 soldiers. The captives he temporarily held were put to death. In his diary entry for August 31, 1526, Suleyman recorded the following statement: "The emperor, seated on a golden throne, receives the homage of the vizirs and beys: massacre of 2,000 prisoners: the rain falls in torrents."[39] Where did Calvin stand on this issue of moral theology? Did he believe that warfare ought to be prosecuted with humanity or in an unsparing way without restraint?

We must now consider the teaching of Calvin on the laws of war in order to surface his own take on the matter of justice in war. The biblical text that is the *locus classicus* on this subject is Deuteronomy 20. On the interpretation of this passage, there was a profound divergence between Calvin and Bullinger. In Zurich, Bullinger proclaimed his position in the most unmistakable terms: "The laws of war are recited in the 20th chapter of Deuteronomy, both profitable and necessary, and therewithal so evident, that they need no words of mine to expound them. Moreover, in every place of scripture these laws of war are still bidden to be kept."[40]

Calvin would have strongly dissented from such a blanket acceptance of the ongoing validity of the entirety of Deuteronomy 20. As to the presentation in this passage of the laws of war pertaining to engagements with foreign powers,[41] Calvin believed that they were far from the law of charity. As to the textual directive regarding the application of holy war to the inhabitants of the land,[42] he affirmed that this was a unique

39. Quoted in Rice and Grafton, *The Foundations of Early Modern Europe*, 137.

40. Sermon 9, *Decades*, 380.

41. Deut 20:10–15.

42. Deut 20:16–18.

event in redemptive history. He believed that the passage was simply teaching that a particular people at a particular time in a particular place were to be judged by God by means of the instrumentality of the Jews.

A key feature in Calvin's interpretation of this crucial Old Testament passage relates to his handling of Deuteronomy 20:12–13, which provided the law of God concerning siege warfare and the requirement of the Lord to massacre all the men of the city who refused to surrender to Israel. In Calvin's political supplement to the sixth commandment, we learn that he was not at all comfortable with the divine mandate that all the men in a city that offered resistance to Israel in a time of war should be killed. On this aspect of the Mosaic political law, Calvin objected that "the permission here given seems to confer too great a license." He asked this question: "Since heathen writers command even the conquered to be spared, and enjoin that those should be admitted to mercy who lay down their arms, and cast themselves on the good faith of the General, although the battering-ram may have actually made a breach in the wall, how does God, the Father of mercies, give His sanction to indiscriminate bloodshed?"[43]

The pagan writer that Calvin appealed to in this statement was Cicero, quoting specifically from his book *On Duties*. Cicero had stated, "And while you must have concern for those whom you have conquered by force, you must also take in those who have laid down their arms and seek refuge in the faith of generals, although a battering ram may have crashed against their wall."[44]

Calvin went on to compare the biblical text at this point with a higher principle, the law of charity. On the one hand,

---

43. *Commentaries on the Last Four Books of Moses*, 53.
44. Cicero, *On Duties*, 15.

"this permission . . . to slaughter, which is extended to all the males, is far distant from perfection." The law of charity, conversely, provided a more perfect standard: "Unquestionably, by the law of charity, even armed men should be spared, if casting away the sword, they crave for mercy."[45] Here Calvin was essentially advocating the law of charity not only in opposition to the biblical text, but also with reference to the standard procedure of siege warfare in the Middle Ages. Once the medieval siege formally began, either with firing of cannons or siege engines, the commander of the besieging forces had every right, according to the law of arms, to show no mercy to any of the soldiers or any other men in the city.[46]

In contrast to Bullinger, Calvin did not accept the idea that the laws of war in Deuteronomy 20 are still to be followed in their entirety by modern governments.[47] In Deuteronomy 20:16–17

---

45. *Commentaries on the Last Four Books of Moses*, 53.

46. Keen, *The Laws of War in the Late Middle Ages*, 120.

47. It should be remembered at this point that Calvin was not a theonomist. He did not believe that the establishment of a modern Christian state required re-institution of the ancient Mosaic civil law. In *Institutes* IV.20.14 he wrote, "I have undertaken to say with what laws a Christian state ought to be governed. . . . I would have preferred to pass over this matter in utter silence if I were not aware that here many dangerously go astray. For there are some who deny that a commonwealth is duly framed which neglects the political system of Moses, and is ruled by the common laws of nations. Let other men consider how perilous and seditious this notion is; it will be enough for me to have proved it false and foolish." Calvin repeated his opposition to a theonomic position with a final statement in *Institutes* IV.20.16: "For the statement of some, that the law of God given through Moses is dishonored when it is abrogated and new laws preferred to it, is utterly vain. . . . For the Lord through the hand of Moses did not give that law to be proclaimed among all nations and to be in force everywhere." Cf., Hesselink, *Calvin's Concept of the Law*, 243–44.

God commanded a complete annihilation of the inhabitants of the land. Calvin believed that the holy war directive given to ancient Israel was a unique event in redemptive history, identifying it as God's special judgment: "God knowing the excessive wickednesse of all those nations to be utterly unreclaimable, determined to take them quite and cleane out of the world." He maintained that "Here therefore, wee must behold Gods speciall judgment."[48]

The exceptional nature of the Jewish holy wars commanded by God in Deuteronomy was underscored by Calvin in three ways. First, the Lord mandated holy war against specific nations. "Our Lorde commaunded all those nations to bee rooted out and to bee put to sworde and havocke without any mercie at all."[49] The people of the land of Canaan were so judged because "the race was accursed and reprobated."[50] Secondly, such an unrestrained method of warfare was to occur in a very specific place, within the boundaries of the land promised to Abraham and his descendants. The unique status of ancient Palestine as the Holy Land had a crucial implication. "Since that land was consecrated to God's service," he argued, "its inhabitants were to be exterminated, who could do nothing but contaminate it."[51] Thirdly, the non-exemplary character of the Deuteronomic holy-war mandate is reflected in the specific instrument of justice chosen by God, namely the Jewish people. In his commentary treatment of Deuteronomy 20:15–18, Calvin stated, "For God had not only armed the Jews to carry on war with them, but

---

48. Sermon 118, *Sermons on Deuteronomy*, 728.

49. Ibid. Calvin even specified some of the nations that were reserved for punishment, referring to the "Amorrhites, Hethites, Chananites, Pheresites, Jebusites, and their like."

50. *Commentaries on the Book of Joshua*, 97.

51. *Commentaries on the Last Four Books of Moses*, 54.

had appointed them to be the ministers and executioners of His vengeance."[52]

We can see that Calvin did not view any of the Old Testament passages that presented the prosecution of holy war as providing justification for the ongoing practice of holy war in the sixteenth century. Calvin knew that holy war was something much different than the medieval Peace of God movement. It deviated from the restraints advocated by the proponents of the *jus in bello*. Holy war entailed "the indiscriminate and promiscuous slaughter, making no distinction of age or sex, but including alike women and children, the aged and the decrepit."[53] As to "how far this doctrine is applicable to us," he declared in no uncertain terms, "To us, in the present day, no certain region marks out our precise boundaries; nor are we armed with the sword to slay all the ungodly."[54] In the teaching of Calvin, the door to the on-going practice of Old Testament holy war remained shut. In Zurich, however, the door was opened slightly by Vermigli, and even more widely by Bullinger.

WARFARE WITHOUT RESTRAINT

Enemies who laid down their arms in battle and who appealed for mercy should be spared. This was the view of Calvin. Although he did not discuss the treatment of captives at any great length, he did speak against their slaughter by asking his congregation this question: "What a thing then is it, when men shalbe put all to the sword without sparing?" He then answered his own enquiry by asking, "Is it not as good as defying God?"[55] He possibly here had in mind the widespread practice in the

52. Ibid., 53–54.
53. *Commentaries on the Book of Joshua*, 97.
54. Ibid., 268.
55. Sermon 119, *Sermons on Deuteronomy*, 734.

Middle Ages of defeated peasant infantry being massacred by the victorious knights.[56] His response to such a practice seems to have been quite straightforward: putting all the captives to death would be to flaunt God himself.

While Calvin briefly addressed the issue, he did not develop the question of what to do with captive soldiers in any significant detail. On this point, Vermigli wrote at length in a *locus* devoted to the subject.[57] He began his discussion by making this statement: "But whether Captives should be slaine, or saved, it cannot be determined in one sentence."[58] He essentially maintained that the issue is highly nuanced. He argued that, if possible, it would be better to spare captives.[59] He did not believe, however, that they ought always to be spared.[60] The policy of mercy was not absolute and universal; there might well be exceptions to the general rule.[61] There were "just occasions," in the view of Vermigli, when captives "must be put to death." To cite one example, the actions of a government depend upon whether the captives are curable or incurable. The incurable should be executed.[62]

While Vermigli contemplated the possibility of exterminating a group of captives, Bullinger envisioned circumstances in which noncombatants, as well as armed soldiers, would be

56. Johnson, *Just War Tradition and the Restraint of War*, 137.

57. Vermigli presented a thorough discussion of the proper treatment of captive soldiers that later was included in a separate chapter in *The Common Places*. See Chapter 18 in Vermigli, *The Common Places*, entitled *Whether Captives ought to be kept or put to death* (IV.18.1–13).

58. *The Common Places* IV.18.1.

59. *The Common Places* IV.18.3.

60. Donnelly, "Peter Martyr Vermigli's Political Ethics," 60–65, provides a brief overview on Vermigli's teaching on war.

61. *The Common Places* IV.18.1.

62. *The Common Places* IV.18.4.

put to death in a time of war. Regarding the civil magistrate, Bullinger explicitly stated that he "of duty is compelled to make war upon men which are incurable, whom the very judgment of the Lord condemneth and biddeth to kill without pity or mercy."[63] Bullinger here spoke about the prosecution of war without humanitarian restraint—that the Lord bids the civil magistrate at times "to kill without pity or mercy." Such unrestrained warfare must be waged against the "incurable." This was the same note sounded by Vermigli, that the incurable must not be spared—a reference to people who had done repeated harm in the past and were expected to do the same in the future. One historical example of such warfare, Bullinger contended, is to be found in the Old Testament book of Numbers in "the wars as Moses had with the Midianites."[64]

As Bullinger well knew, Numbers 31 records the execution of noncombatants—captive Midianite women and male infants. Killing "without pity or mercy" meant violating the limits of war traditionally developed in the doctrine of *jus in bello*. In these statements, Bullinger was drawing away from the medieval Peace of God trajectory, which culminated in later just war teaching. In a real sense, his teaching at this point could have provided a justification for the massacre of Irish combatants and noncombatants alike under Cromwell's Puritan army at Drogheda.

In the ancient biblical world, killing without pity or mercy is seen in the wars of Moses against the Midianites. The same thing, Bullinger affirmed, applies to the present time: "Such are at this day those arrogant and seditious rebels as trouble commonweals and kingdoms."[65] In this statement, Bullinger appears

63. Sermon 9, *Decades*, 376.
64. Ibid.
65. Ibid.

to have affirmed that with respect to rebels, the people responsible for sedition, there must be no pity. The absence of all mercy would surely mean that for a rebel to cast away arms and appeal for mercy would be a useless endeavor.

Unlike the Zurich tradition in Bullinger and Vermigli, which paved the way for holy war ideas and practice in the English Civil War, Calvin stood without wavering in the medieval just war tradition. When a state determined that a given war was morally justified, it also had to be concerned, said Calvin, about godly warfare and the moral obligation of justice in war.

4

Warring by the Popular Magistrates

THE TYRANT, in the view of Calvin, was the opposite of the good magistrate who was a "guardian of peace" and a "protector of righteousness."[1] The tyrant was a "savage prince."[2] The tyrant sees to it, observed Calvin, that "all liberty shall be taken away." Specifically, "tyrannical violence" sees to it that "no freedom of speech" is "allowed." "Tyrants would impose silence on all teachers" who would dare to bring a word of reproof against them—"now throwing them into prisons, then banishing them."[3] Such rulers were known for "plundering houses, raping virgins and matrons, and slaughtering the innocent."[4] They were the "kings who violently fall upon and assault the lowly common folk."[5]

This understanding of the tyrant as one who tramples upon the people had been articulated by Salisbury, who made the point that the tyrant "reduces the people to slavery."[6] Salisbury had also portrayed the tyrant in terms of his relationship to law—which he identified as "the gift of God, the model of equity, a standard

1. *Institutes* IV.20.24.
2. *Institutes* IV.20.29.
3. *Commentaries on the Prophet Amos*, 269–70.
4. *Institutes* IV.20.24.
5. *Institutes* IV.20.31.
6. *Policraticus* VIII.17.

of justice, a likeness of the Divine Will" and "the guardian of well-being." In contrast to the prince who "fights for the laws and the liberty of the people," the "tyrant thinks nothing done unless he brings the laws to nothing."[7]

This perspective on the nature of tyranny, explaining it in terms of its relationship to law, was picked up by the Reformed in the sixteenth century. Bullinger, for example, defined a tyrant as a prince who believes that he is the source of the law and therefore may create law according to what he fancies.[8] Bad magistrates think that they may do as they please with the laws—"they may turn, put out, undo, make and unmake, them as they list at their pleasure."[9] The good magistrate, contended Bullinger, has a much different perspective. For such a prince, the law is an objective standard to which he submits himself.[10]

The reflections of Theodore Beza upon the issue of tyranny in *Concerning the Rights of Rulers* were his direct response to the St. Bartholomew massacres, which began on August 24, 1572.[11] The wholesale slaughter of Huguenots in Paris and throughout France was ultimately caused by the tyrannical determination of King Charles IX to murder the Admiral of France, Gaspard de Coligny, and some two or three dozen members of the Huguenot nobility who were still in Paris following the wedding of Henry of Navarre and Marguerite of Valois. With a tyrant upon the royal throne of France, Beza completed a draft of his political treatise by July of 1573.

7. Ibid.

8. "One specie" of tyranny occurs, wrote the Reformed jurist Althusius, *Politica*, 192, when the magistrate "violates, changes, or overthrows the fundamental laws of the realm."

9. Sermon 7, *Decades*, 339.

10. Ibid.

11. Kingdon, "Reactions to the St. Bartholomew Massacres," 30; Gosselin, "David in *Tempore Belli*," 33, 36.

What then, in the thinking of Beza, was tyranny? He expressed ideas that had been articulated by theologians in the medieval period and in his own time by Calvin and the Reformed. Tyranny relates to the issue of opposition to law, he maintained. It is "authority setting itself against the laws."[12] "Its peculiar concomitant is a persistent malice which strives with might and maim to subvert the constitution and the laws upon which the kingdom rests as upon foundations."[13] The tyrant is also a man who destroys his subjects. "Tyrants," he said, "do not strive to have subjects in their power for any other reason but to persecute and crush them to their destruction."[14] In addition, tyrannical madness can have a religious dimension to it. Beza described tyranny as "assailing the true religion and even stamping it out as far as may be."[15]

Tyranny, then, was an evil to which Calvin, along with the medievals and the Reformed, gave studious attention. There were remedies, though, in Calvin's thought for despotic governments. In the first place, the private individual was to pray.[16] Such prayer might well lead to the second remedy of divine intervention by means of a servant avenger, a brave man who would deliver the distressed.[17] The third remedy for tyranny was an institutional one. Here Calvin appealed to the existence of the *populares magistratus* in *Institutes* IV.20.31, calling them "magistrates of the people, appointed to restrain the willfulness of kings."[18]

12. *Concerning the Rights of Rulers*, 48.
13. Ibid., 80.
14. Ibid., 70.
15. Ibid., 82.
16. *Institutes* IV.20.29.
17. *Institutes* IV.20.30.
18. See *Calvini Opera*, vol. 2, col. 1116.

PARLIAMENTARY RESISTANCE

It needs to be stressed that Calvin did not use the expression *inferiores magistratus* in this classic passage. Skinner even contends that "Calvin never alluded to the concept of inferior magistrates in this (or any other) discussion about political resistance."[19] Beza, on the other hand, wrote at length about the inferior magistrates in *De jure magistratum* in *Quaestio* VI.[20] In the thinking of Beza, the inferior magistrates were individuals who ruled on more of a local level. They gave their attention to local government, exercising authority over a limited area. With reference to France, he provided clear identification as to who the inferior magistrates were. The first type would be "dukes, marquises, counts, viscounts, barons and squires."[21] This group would be the aristocrats.[22] The second would be "majors, vicars, consuls, capitolini (municipal judges), syndics, scabini (alderman) and the like."[23] This group would be rulers of cities who had been elected to office.[24]

The existence of the inferior magistrates in France made provision for resistance against a possible abuse of the monarch's military power: "All magistrates are obliged to thwart tyranny on an interim basis by defending persons within their jurisdiction against the unjust exercise of power by the central authority."[25] Such a defense, of course, would necessarily entail the taking up

---

19. Skinner, *The Foundations of Modern Political Thought*, 2:232.
20. See the Latin reading in *De jure magistratum*, 41.
21. *Concerning the Rights of Rulers*, 39.
22. Kingdon, *Myths about the St. Bartholomew's Day Massacres,* 157.
23. *Concerning the Rights of Rulers*, 39.
24. Kingdon, *Myths about St. Bartholomew's Day Massacres*, 157.
25. *Concerning the Rights of Rulers*, 46.

of arms by the inferior magistrates, and Beza maintained that this was their duty.[26]

It is important to recognize that the inferior magistrates in Beza's conception had the right to engage in a *defensive war* against monarchical tyranny. They were authorized to take up arms against the armies of the prince who would seek to exterminate them. This was the same position that Luther had articulated in his *Warning to His Dear German People*. Like Luther, Beza took the view that the inferior magistrates did not have the authority to act proactively—that is, they did not have the right to move against and to depose, and even to execute a king.[27] Beza differed in this respect from the teaching of the Strasbourg Reformer Martin Bucer who had argued in his *Explications of the Four Gospels* that the inferior magistrates—self-governing city authorities and territorial princes—held the power of the sword not only to defend their people against a "godless tyrant" who might fall upon them, but also had the right to "attempt to remove him by force of arms."[28]

Beza's teaching at this point, in which he authorized the inferior magistrates to resist tyranny, would have provided a theological defense for the Reformed in the French Civil Wars.

---

26. Ibid., 41. In *Quaestio* VII, Beza qualified his call to armed resistance with three axioms. First, "the tyranny must be undisguised and notorious." Secondly, "recourse should not be had to arms before all other remedies have been tried." Thirdly, this recourse to arms should not be had "before the question has been thoroughly examined, not only as to what is permissible, but also as to what is expedient, lest the remedies prove more hazardous than the very disease" (73–74). Later, in *Quaestio* VIII, he provided this maxim: "It befits a wise man to make trial of all things by deliberation before armed force" (80).

27. *Concerning the Rights of Rulers*, 75.

28. Quoted in Skinner, *The Foundations of Modern Political Thought*, 2:206.

The mere fact that the French aristocracy and city rulers were not passively going to lay down their necks at Catholic chopping blocks meant that the Wars of Religion would last for as long as the Catholic majority sought to stamp out the Reformed faith in France. Eventually, after almost four decades of struggle in the "long and horrendous" series of Wars of Religion, the efforts of the Protestant forces paid off in the Edict of Nantes, which granted legal standing to the Reformed faith in certain areas of France.[29]

As we have noted, while Beza and Bucer among the Reformed wrote at length about the role of the inferior magistrates in taking up arms in defense of their people against a tyrannical prince, Calvin did not refer to inferior magistrates in his classic treatment of resistance in the *Institutes*. It is a correct conception to maintain that in the *Institutes* the place of Bucer's *inferior magistrates* is taken by the *magistrates of the people*—as Calvin put it, the *populares magistratus*.[30] It has been well stated that "the Latin *populares* was a term quite different in connotation from 'inferior' or 'lesser.'"[31] The idea in the expression *populares magistratus* was that these individuals constituted a representative body that was appointed in an elective manner.[32]

---

29. Labrousse, *Bayle*, 1. Munck, *Seventeenth Century Europe*, 41, states that the Huguenots "were granted some 900 places of worship, with rights to hold services on the estates of Protestant noblemen and in places where Huguenot worship had occurred in 1596 and 1597."

30. Baron, "Was Calvin's Thought the Inspiration for the Earliest Democratic Revolts in Europe?" 53.

31. Höpfl makes this statement in *Luther and Calvin on Secular Authority*, 82, note 104.

32. Höpfl makes the observation that "Calvin habitually uses the republican word *magistratus*." This term, he contends, "more definitely intimates the elective manner of appointment" (Ibid., xli).

Calvin left his readers with no ambiguity as to the kind of representative assembly he had in mind: "As in ancient times the ephors were set against the Spartan kings, or the tribunes of the people against the Roman consuls, or the demarchs against the senate of the Athenians; and perhaps, as things now are, such power as the three estates exercise in every realm when they hold their chief assemblies."[33] Here Calvin appealed to both history and to contemporary political theory. Among the ancient Greeks and Romans, he drew attention to individuals who were appointed in an elective manner—the *ephori*, *tribuni plebes*, and *demarchi*.[34] With respect to his own time, he alluded to the various European parliamentary bodies.[35] His reference to the "three estates" no doubt included the French Estates-General, composed of the clergy (the First Estate), the nobles (the Second Estate), and the burghers or townsmen (the Third Estate). The convening of the French Estates-General entailed the election of deputies by each of the respective estates.[36]

---

33. *Institutes* IV.20.31.

34. Skinner, *The Foundations of Modern Political Thought*, 2:232.

35. Graham, *The Constructive Revolutionary*, 53.

36. Skinner, *The Foundations of Modern Political Thought*, 2:233. King Philip the Fair convened the first Estates-General in 1302. The elective principle first came into full play in the meeting of the Estates-General in 1484. Baumgartner, *France in the Sixteenth Century*, 11, writes concerning this: "In October 1483 letters went out convoking the Estates at Tours. The letters contained a major innovation in the manner of choosing who would attend. Instead of the king naming the deputies for the clergy and nobility and the municipal governments electing their delegates, the local royal officials were told to assemble the members of each estate in their districts, of which there were about 100 in the realm, to elect a deputy to represent their respective estates. The new procedure produced a body of deputies who were more responsive to their constituents." Cf. Baumgartner, *Change and Continuity in the French Episcopate*, 97.

Popular magistrates—in other words, parliamentary bodies—had the duty to "withstand . . . the fierce licentiousness of kings . . . who violently fall upon and assault the lowly common people."[37] In a lengthy sentence of eighty-eight Latin words,[38] Calvin included three elements at the basis of his appeal to the popular magistrates of his time that they must protect the lives and freedom of the people: the historical, the legal, and the theological.[39] Earlier, on the issue of the authority to take up arms, Calvin had used the theological element—indeed, he had rested his case upon the Scripture itself. As to the authority of the prince to take up arms in defense of the commonwealth, Calvin had declared, "And the Holy Spirit declares such wars to be lawful by many testimonies of Scripture."[40] Here, when he discussed the taking up of arms by the popular magistrates, Calvin once again included the scriptural allusion, maintaining that such officers "have been appointed protectors by God's ordinance."[41] There was also, however, what Skinner calls a "secular and constitutional element" that was introduced into his discussion.[42] As Walzer writes, "Against the fact of Catholic monarchy in France . . . Calvin struggled to set a *counter-fact*, an opposing force as real . . . as ordinary as tyranny itself—the power of the Protestant nobility."[43]

37. *Institutes* IV.20.31.
38. *Calvini Opera*, vol. 2, col. 1116.
39. Skinner, *The Foundations of Modern Political Thought*, 2:234.
40. *Institutes* IV.20.11.
41. *Institutes* IV.20.31.
42. Skinner, *The Foundations of Modern Political Thought*, 2:233.
43. Walzer, *The Revolution of the Saints*, 59.

THE MEDIEVAL HERITAGE

Although the Reformed for generations have looked to Calvin for a theological justification for armed resistance to tyranny, his doctrine was by no means entirely new.[44] Walzer notes, "That nobles might act to bridle the king was an old medieval idea."[45] A specific instance of this is seen in the *Magna Carta* of 1215, in which King John conceded that a baronial committee should be set up to hear complaints and that it should, furthermore, have the authority to wage war against the king if he failed to give redress.[46] In 1258 the principle of a baronial war against the king came to fruition in the uprising led by Simon de Montfort, who led the barons to victory over the royal army.

In a general sense, key medieval thinkers affirmed that the right to make war was by no means restricted to the king or the prince. Christine de Pisan in her book *Livre des Fays d'Armes et de Chevalerie* stated, "And without a doubt, according to law and right, the right to do battle or levy war for any cause whatever belongs to sovereign princes, such as Emperors, Kings, Dukes, and other secular lords principal of secular jurisdiction."[47] To cite another example, Aquinas moved the discussion along toward the possibility of a civil war that might legitimately result from tyrannical actions by a monarch. He first cautioned that "to proceed against the cruelty of tyrants is an action to be undertaken, not through private presumption of a few, but rather by public authority."[48] He then moved to an explanation as to why one government body could legitimately raise arms against

---

44. Foster, "Calvin and His Followers Championed Representative Government," 44.

45. Walzer, *The Revolution of the Saints*, 60.

46. Stephenson, *Mediæval History*, 477–78.

47. Quoted in Keen, *The Laws of War in the Late Middle Ages*, 77.

48. *On Kingship, to the King of Cyprus* I.6.48.

the king: "If to provide itself with a king belongs to the right of a given multitude, it is not unjust that the king be deposed or have his power restricted by that same multitude if, becoming a tyrant, he abuses the royal power."[49] Aquinas then went on to show that such a perspective was not merely a thirteenth-century perspective: "Thus did the Romans. . . . Domitian . . . was slain by the Roman senate when he exercised tyranny."[50] In the view of Aquinas, nothing could be more rational and just: The public authority that places a man into kingship had the right to remove him from power, if he should lapse into tyranny.

THE CONCURRENCE OF THE REFORMED

The position of Aquinas at this point was revived in the political theory of Vermigli, who justified war against a tyrant on the same basis. Like Calvin, Vermigli drew attention to ancient political arrangements, mentioning both the ephors and the tribunes. While Calvin stated that the ephors "were set against" the Spartan kings and the tribunes "against" the consuls, Vermigli included the perspective that the kings and the consuls were "in a manner dependeth of them."[51] The ephors and tribunes "in verie deede doe elect" the kings and consuls.[52] In addition to this, while Calvin merely referred to kings and popular magistrates, Vermigli added the nuance that the kings were the "superiour powers" and the bodies that elected them were "inferiour unto princes."[53] In a move reminiscent of Aquinas, he drew an irresistible conclusion from the fact that parliamentary bodies put a man into kingship: The principle of installation brings with

49. *On Kingship, to the King of Cyprus* I.6.49.
50. Ibid.
51. *The Common Places* IV.21.12.
52. Ibid.
53. Ibid.

it the principle of deposition. Vermigli wrote concerning the inferior powers, "To these undoubtedly if the prince performe not his covenants and promises, it is lawfull to constrain and bring him into order, and by force to compel him to perfourme the conditions and covenaunts which he had promised, and that by warre, when it cannot otherwise be done."[54]

As we apply this principle to the events of the sixteenth century, we are reminded of a major difference between Reformed and Lutheran thinking in the area of political doctrine. Even as Vermigli approved of the deposition of King Christian II by the inferior magistrates in Denmark,[55] Luther firmly repudiated the deposition in his treatise *Whether Soldiers, Too, Can Be Saved*. He based his position upon his reading of Romans 13. "No one shall fight or make war against his overlord," he argued, "for a man owes his overlord obedience, honor, fear."[56] Although Luther was willing to consider the question as to whether or not there might be an exception to this fundamental law, he no sooner introduced the question than he followed with his own colorful answer. "What I say about 'subjects,'" Luther specified, "is intended for peasants, citizens of the cities, nobles, counts, and princes as well." He then warned that "a rebellious noble, count, or prince should have his head cut off the same as a rebellious peasant."[57]

As we have already noted, Beza stood in continuity with the Lutheran tradition that the monarch's power is limited by the inferior magistrates. Beza picked up the idea espoused by Luther that, in Hendrix's words, "Protestant princes could rightfully re-

54. Ibid.
55. *The Common Places* IV.21.13.
56. *Whether Soldiers, Too, Can Be Saved*, 103.
57. Ibid., 116.

sist the emperor with force should he move against them."[58] It made sense that "evangelical preaching must be defended and that resisting those who sought to suppress it was allowable (even honorable)."[59] Beza, however, did not agree with Luther in terms of his opposition to the idea of a parliamentary body moving against a king and removing him from office. In addition to the inferior magistrate who provided for a vertical distribution of power in a nation, Beza affirmed a second institutional way in which the authority of the prince ought to be limited. The Estates-General provided for a horizontal distribution of authority. While Calvin briefly referred to this institution in one sentence at the conclusion of the *Institutes*, Beza expounded at length upon the subject of the Estates of the People.[60]

Beza located this institution within the Old Testament history of Israel.[61] The Estates of ancient Israel had a three-fold authority. They had the right to choose a king, but they could also depose him and even punish him: "The . . . Estates of the people of Israel had authority to choose for themselves from the family of David whom they wished, and afterwards, when he had been elected, either to drive him out or even to execute sentence of death upon him as the occasion demanded."[62] As an example of a biblical deposition and execution, Beza cited the uprising of the people of Judah against King Amaziah, resulting in his execution, which was followed by the installation of his son Azariah in his place.[63] He maintained that this was done "in

58. Hendrix, "Luther," 49.

59. Whitford, *Tyranny and Resistance*, 12.

60. Note Beza's discussion on the *Estats de leur Peuples* in *Du droit des magistratus*, 39.

61. Beza referred to the Estates in Israel as "les Estats de ce people" and "les Estats du Roiaume" (*Du droit des magistrates*, 31).

62. *Concerning the Rights of Rulers*, 52.

63. Ibid., 51–52.

accordance with the resolution and studied deliberation of the people of Jerusalem."[64]

When Beza wrote about the *Estats de leur Peuples* in France, he was speaking, of course, about the Estates-General. He believed that the Estates ought to have a significant role in government. This is reflected in his discussion of the Kingdom of England, which he called "the most blessed of all . . . in the whole world."[65] He clearly approved of the political structure in England, which involved a real horizontal distribution of power between the monarchy and the Parliament. He made the remark that "nearly all authority of government is dependent upon the consent of Parliament."[66] Beza wanted the same kind of arrangement in France. The Estates-General were to be advisors of the king so that the monarch would be "directed and advised by" them.[67]

The Estates-General also had the significant power of deposing and even punishing a king. Beza argued the right of deposition both logically and historically. He maintained that the Estates "conferred the principal positions of dignity and high office in the Kingdom."[68] His fundamental premise, in continuity with Aquinas, was that "those who possess authority to elect a king . . . also have the right to dethrone him."[69] He also argued his case by appealing to French history, maintaining that the "Estates had the power of dismissing the kings whom they had elected if they committed any wrong."[70] He declared

64. Ibid., 52. When Beza referred to "la deliberation de ceux de Jerusalem," he was not describing the private individuals of Jerusalem, but rather the Estates (*Du droit des magistrates*, 31).

65. Ibid., 53.
66. Ibid.
67. Ibid.
68. Ibid., 60.
69. Ibid., 64.
70. Ibid., 59–60.

that there were "countless examples" of kings in France who had been deposed, starting with such ancient disgraced monarchs as Chilperic and Theodoric.[71] Finally, Beza affirmed that the deposition of a king might well, at certain times, go one step further. The Estates-General also had the power of punishment: "The Estates . . . can and must . . . oppose the tyrant and even, if need be, inflict just and deserved punishment upon him."[72]

The preceding discussion has demonstrated that Protestant political thought on the issue of parliamentary resistance to tyrannical government was divided. On the far right was Luther.[73] "Wars and uprisings against our superiors cannot be right," he wrote.[74] Bullinger stood with Luther on this point. For Bullinger, "there was no effective human check on magisterial power."[75] Standing more in the mainstream of the medieval tradition reflected in Aquinas were Calvin and Vermigli—each essentially embracing a parliamentary check upon kingly authority. While Calvin alluded to the French Estates-General, Vermigli referred to the Electors of the Holy Roman Emperor. The teaching of Beza on the Estates of the People amounted to an elaboration of Calvin's succinct statement on the popular magistrates and the three estates. It was likewise in continuity with Vermigli's teaching on the inferior powers, which referred, in his thinking, to European parliaments that could elect princes and remove them from authority.

71. Ibid., 60.

72. Ibid., 63.

73. Hendrix, "Luther," 49, correctly states that "Luther never endorsed the use of violence by Christians in rebellion against their rulers, even for the sake of a more just and nominally Christian society."

74. *Whether Soldiers, Too, Can Be Saved*, 118.

75. Baker, "Covenant and Community in the Thought of Heinrich Bullinger," 23.

5

The Justice of War

CALVIN, as we have seen, constructed his doctrine on the proper authority for waging war in continuity with the just war tradition that had been established by Augustine of Hippo. With respect to the other elements of the Augustinian tradition, just cause and right intention, he remained quite traditional and conservative.[1] He did go beyond Aquinas in stressing that war must be an option of last resort. There were no substantial differences between Calvin and the Zurich theologians on these issues relating to the justice of war. He differed somewhat, though, from Luther, who deviated from the just war tradition slightly when he spoke against the defense of the Christian faith as part of the just cause.[2]

---

1. Klempa, "War and Peace in Puritan Thought," 85–86, states that Calvin "for the most part" stands in the just war tradition. The problem here is the phrase of qualification; the fact is that Calvin completely stands in the classical medieval tradition arising in Augustine and continuing through Aquinas.

2. In his treatise *On War against the Turk*, Luther wrote that the Emperor was "to defend his own" (184), that he was "to protect his subjects" (185). He was not, however, the "defender of the gospel or the faith," for "the church and the faith must have a defender other than the emperor and kings" (186–87).

A LEGITIMATE CAUSE

After Calvin dealt with the issue of the proper authority for the waging of war, he moved to the matter of just cause, expressing his concern for *legitima bella*: "But kings and people must sometimes take up arms to execute public vengeance. On this basis we may judge wars lawful which are so undertaken."[3] Here Calvin affirmed that there is a standard by which wars may be judged as to whether or not they are lawful. The criterion relates to whether or not the cause of the war is "to execute public vengeance." The need for public vengeance assumes that a fault exists, that wrongdoing has been committed. Some evils that Calvin mentioned included the disturbing of "the common tranquility of all," the raising of "seditious tumults," and "vile misdeeds."[4]

The concern of Calvin for public vengeance makes him sound like Salisbury, who wrote about the duty of soldiers, affirming that "two-edged swords are in their hands to execute punishment on the nations."[5] Luther, likewise, stressed the same point when he asked, "What else is war but the punishment of wrong and evil?"[6] Salisbury and Luther, along with Calvin, were merely reflecting the stand of Augustine, who commented, "The real evils in war are love of violence, revengeful cruelty, fierce and implacable enmity, wild resistance, and the lust of power, and such like; and it is generally to punish these things . . . that . . . good men undertake wars."[7]

In this development, Calvin gave specifics, whereas Aquinas had laid down the more general principle that "those who are attacked, should be attacked because they deserve it on account of

3. *Institutes* IV.20.11. Cf. *Calvini Opera*, vol. 2, col. 1102.
4. *Institutes* IV.20.11.
5. *Policraticus* VI.8.
6. *Whether Soldiers, Too, Can Be Saved*, 95.
7. *Reply to Faustus the Manichean* XXII.74.

some fault."[8] Aquinas, however, alluded to a specific fault when he referred to that which a nation had "seized unjustly."[9] This was obviously a reference to an invasion, the naked aggression of one nation against another. It was an issue that he elaborated upon in his discussion of warfare and holy days. He argued from the lesser to the greater in his contention that there are times when fighting must occur on such days:

> Physicians may lawfully attend to their patients on holy days. Now there is much more reason for safeguarding the common weal (whereby many are saved from being slain, and innumerable evils both temporal and spiritual prevented), than the bodily safety of an individual. Therefore, for the purpose of safeguarding the common weal of the faithful, it is lawful to carry on a war on holy days, provided there be need for doing so.[10]

It is true that Aquinas regarded the just war as being a defense of the community.[11] It should also be noted though that Aquinas referred in this passage to "safeguarding the common weal *of the faithful.*" The just war entailed the protection of the *reipublicae fidelium.*[12] Obviously, to defend the commonwealth of the faithful—which is one of the bases for a just war—necessarily entailed the defense of the freedom to practice the Christian religion in public. Every defensive war is in fact a safeguarding

---

8. *Summa Theologica* 2a2ae, q. 40, art. 1.

9. Ibid.

10. *Summa Theologica* 2a2ae, q. 40, art. 4.

11. Russell, *The Just War in the Middle Ages*, 290.

12. *Summa Theologica* 2a2ae, q. 40, art. 4. The Latin text of this passage is provided in Aquinas, *Summa Theologiae*, 92.

of all the fundamental constituents of liberty, which includes the right to practice the true religion in its purity.[13]

Calvin agreed with the conception that the commonwealth of the faithful had to be defended by the civil authority. "Princes must be armed," he said, "to defend by war the dominions entrusted to their safekeeping, if at any time they are under enemy attack."[14] He took the view that such defensive wars were not only morally permissible, but even obligatory. In his public preaching on Deuteronomy 20, Calvin declared, "And as a Judge ought to punishe a theefe or a robber: so likewise they that have the power ordeyned of God, may enter into armes against all such as fall to troubling and vexing of their subjectes, and such manner of warres are not onely lawfull but also of necessitie to be undertaken by them."[15] In his more concise commentary treatment of the same biblical text, Calvin made the case that "the unjust aggression of their enemies" would have provided a "legitimate cause" for Israel "to engage in war."[16] In other words, a defensive war is morally legitimate. In his fuller, more expanded sermonic exposition, we observe that a defensive war is morally necessary.

---

13. Pace Bainton the conception that "fighting for religion" places a military engagement in the category of a holy war is not correct (*Christian Attitudes toward War and Peace*, 149.) Full-fledged holy war has two defining constituents: It is authorized and initiated by the church, and it is prosecuted without humanitarian restraint. It should be stressed that no theologians among the Reformed embraced holy war doctrine in its entirety. Some of the Reformed accepted the second constituent of holy war teaching in their disregard of medieval justice-in-war doctrine concerning the protection of noncombatants.

14. *Institutes* IV.20.11.

15. Sermon 116, *Sermons on Deuteronomy*, 711.

16. *Commentaries on the Last Four Books of Moses*, 102.

We also learn in his sermons on 2 Samuel that a defensive war protects not only the liberty of the commonwealth, but also the true religion that flourishes within it. Calvin affirmed that "men will never have a just cause for waging war except for the common good and conservation of the public condition, or for the honour of God."[17] He later expanded upon this line of thinking: "The two bases for a just war among men are for the honor and worship of God and for the safety of all the people . . . that the honour of God be maintained, and religion kept in its purity and, secondly, that the people be maintained in peace."[18] It should here be observed that Calvin did not distinguish between a just cause and a holy cause (which is religion).[19] For Calvin the defense of religion was as much a just cause as the defense of the public peace. Aquinas likewise had spoken about "safeguarding the common weal of the faithful" in the context of a discussion on just war doctrine. Thus it was that Calvin affirmed that the Christian commonwealth—God's "sovereign empire" where "all people" give "homage to him"—is to be maintained by "those who rule and whom God has chosen to bear the sword."[20]

Beza believed along with Calvin that a defensive war was not only permissible, but even obligatory. Commenting upon the Old Testament history, Beza wrote, "I maintain that the Israelites were free not merely to disobey the sinful commands of these peoples but even to set a just defence against their unjust violence, and that therefore the leaders of the tribes (*of Israel*) did a grievous wrong whenever they omitted to oppose

17. Sermon 30, *Sermons on 2 Samuel*, 458.

18. Sermon 31, *Sermons on 2 Samuel*, 461.

19. Bainton, "Congregationalism and the Puritan Revolution from the Just War to the Crusade," 250, makes such a distinction between a just cause and a holy cause. Cf. Bainton, *Christian Attitudes toward War and Peace*, 148.

20. Sermon 31, *Sermons on 2 Samuel*, 461.

the foreign foe with united courage and strength in defence of the liberty of their country."[21] Like Calvin, he recognized that a defensive war against a foreign invader had the two constituents of protecting the public order of the commonwealth and the true religion that was practiced in it: "It admits of no doubt that even private individuals are bound by the law of God and men to succour with all their power their country when oppressed and in distress, especially however when its religion and liberty are simultaneously endangered."[22]

Like Aquinas in the medieval period and in continuity with Calvin and Beza in Geneva, Bullinger and Vermigli asserted that the defense of the commonwealth and true religion are two bases when it comes to the matter of just causes for war. On the one hand, Bullinger spoke about "the defence of true religion."[23] It was "lawful" for the magistrates "to defend the Church."[24] On the other hand, the magistrate must also "defend with the sword" the things of this life—"liberty, wealth, chastity, and his subjects' bodies."[25] Bullinger not only talked about these two bases relative to just cause separately, but also together. He intertwined the secular and the religious issues when he referred to "the defence of religion, of the laws of God, of his country, wife, and children."[26] His colleague took the same approach. Vermigli believed that the magistrate was to defend the commonwealth and the true religion, "the Commonweale and the ordinaunce of God."[27] Reflecting upon the prince and his duty,

21. *Concerning the Rights of Rulers*, 32.
22. Ibid.
23. Sermon 9, *Decades*, 376.
24. Ibid., 377.
25. Ibid., 376–77.
26. Ibid., 379.
27. *The Common Places* IV.17.11.

he affirmed, "He ought in no wise to seeke his owne but the glorie of God and safetie of the Church: and especially if the enemie be such, as mindeth either to destroy or pervert the worshipping of God."[28]

TO SECURE THE PEACE

A just war in the Augustinian tradition required not only authorization by the civil authority and a just cause, but also a right intention. Augustine had affirmed that "the soldiers should perform their military duties in behalf of the peace and safety of the community."[29] Aquinas later stated that a just war must have a "rightful intention," which he explained in terms of seeking "the advancement of good" and as having the "object of securing peace."[30] Luther reflected the same traditional sentiment in his statement that the one who goes to war does so "because he desires peace and obedience."[31] The Zurich theologians expressed themselves similarly. Bullinger contended that they that "enter into warfare" must have a "mark for them all to shoot at." Valiant men of old "warred and went to battle" setting their hearts upon "justice, public-peace, defence to truth and innocency."[32] Vermigli expressed his view in a memorable antithetical statement: "Insomuch as peace is not ordained for warre sake, but warre is taken in hand for peace sake."[33] An examination of Calvin in his biblical commentary work shows that he likewise embraced the third traditional constituent related to the justice of war.

28. Ibid.
29. *Reply to Faustus the Manichean* XXII.74.
30. *Summa Theologica* 2a2ae, q. 40, art. 1.
31. *Whether Soldiers, Too, Can Be Saved*, 95.
32. Sermon 9, *Decades*, 379.
33. *The Common Places* IV.17.21.

In his treatment of war in the *Institutes*, Calvin reflected the disputational form that characterized medieval scholastic theology. His discussion included an *objectio*, which Calvin presented in this dependent clause: "But if anyone object against me that in the New Testament there exists no testimony or example which teaches that war is a thing lawful for Christians."[34] He then set forth three points in his *responsio*. He first reminded his readers that the New Testament has no prohibition against a just war.[35] He then maintained that the burden of proof was not upon himself—that to look for such an explicit statement in the New Testament was to look in the wrong place, for the apostolic writings did not have as their purpose "to fashion a civil government, but to establish the spiritual Kingdom of Christ."[36] Finally, in the third point of his *responsio*, he declared that the New Testament is not silent or irrelevant on this issue. At this point he made an appeal to what had long been a classic text in just war discussion, Luke 3:14.

Calvin, like the medieval exegetes, appealed to the counsel that John the Baptist had given to the soldiers who enquired of him as to their moral duty.[37] Quoting from Luke 3:14, which is

34. *Institutes* IV.20.12.

35. Ibid.

36. Ibid.

37. Augustine had put stress upon the response of John. Having first declared his position that "good men" must at times "undertake wars" and that "right conduct" in certain situations "requires them to act," Augustine appealed to the message that the Baptist delivered to the soldiers who were enquiring concerning the way of salvation: "Otherwise John . . . would have replied, 'Throw away your arms; give up the service; never strike, or wound, or disable anyone.' But knowing that such actions in battle were not murderous, but authorized by law, and that the soldiers did not thus avenge themselves, but defend the public safety, he replied, 'Do violence to no man, accuse no man falsely, and be content with your wages'" (*Reply to Faustus the Manichean* XXII.74). The discussion

referenced in the margin of the 1559 edition that was published in Geneva, Calvin wrote, "But they were told: 'Strike no man, do no man wrong, be content with your wages.' When he taught them to be content with their wages, he certainly did not forbid them to bear arms."

The marginal textual citation in the 1559 *Institutes* may well be a cross-reference to Calvin's biblical commentary on the same passage—Luke 3:14.[38] His commentary on the synoptic gospels had appeared in 1555 in Latin and French.[39] Calvin may have been directing his readers to his fuller discussion of just war doctrine in his biblical commentary. Indeed, his commentary discussion at this point is much more extensive than the very brief exposition in the *Institutes*. In the commentary he expanded upon what John actually forbade, and he argued that this text actually approves of the civil magistrate, containing "an approbation of civil government."[40] He reasoned further that since this passage favors civil government, it necessarily provides an approbation of everything that civil government entails: "Magistrates require not only an executioner, but other attendants, among whom are the military, without whose assistance and agency it is impossible to maintain peace."

The exposition of Luke 3:14 in the biblical commentary has even more significance, though, because of the fact that Calvin here provided the third constituent of Augustinian thought on the justice of war. Calvin drew attention to the matter of right intention when he insisted that "the object must be considered."

---

in *Summa Theologica* 2a2ae, q. 40, art. 1, is instructive. Aquinas first presented four common objections against the lawfulness of war. He then turned to his response. The very first biblical text he appealed to was Luke 3:14, regarding which his interpretation resembled Augustine's.

38. Muller, *The Unaccommodated Calvin*, 107.

39. Greef, *The Writings of John Calvin*, 100.

40. *Commentary on a Harmony of the Evangelists*, 195.

He warned, "Princes must not allow themselves to sport with human blood, nor must soldiers give themselves up to cruelty, from a desire of gain, as if slaughter were their chief business: but both must be drawn to it by necessity, and by a regard for public advantage."[41] Here we are warned that in Calvin scholarship we must beware of the view that there is nothing in the commentaries that does not appear in the *Institutes*. In his discussion of the just war in *Institutes* IV.20.11, Calvin included only the first two of the classical three constituents of a just war.[42] It is only in his commentary on Luke 3:14 that Calvin showed explicit continuity with Augustine and Aquinas—including the third constituent of a just war, that the object must be the advancement of good.

THE LAST RESORT

A just war included three necessary elements. At the foundational level, it had to be initiated by the proper civil authority. It also had to have a just cause and a right intention. Calvin and the Reformed stood in continuity with the traditional teaching. They added, however, a fourth constituent pertaining to the

---

41. Ibid.

42. It is true that there is a vague allusion to Aquinas' third constituent of a just war in *Institutes* IV.20.12 in the statement that "we must perform much more than the heathen philosopher required when he wanted war to seem a seeking of peace." Here Calvin was referring to Cicero's *On Duties* I.35. It is interesting that in his biblical commentary on Deuteronomy 20:10, one of his political supplements to the sixth commandment, Calvin referred to the ancient Roman Cicero by name, and in a positive way: "And that sentiment of Cicero is worthy of praise, 'that wars must not be undertaken except that we may live in unmolested peace'" (*Commentaries on the Last Four Books of Moses*, 52). In this statement Calvin essentially announced his commitment to the third constituent of Augustinian just war theory.

justice of war by maintaining that the waging of war had to be an act of last resort.[43]

Calvin staked out his position in the clearest terms: "If they must arm themselves against the enemy, that is, the armed robber, let them not lightly seek occasion to do so: indeed, let them not accept the occasion when offered, unless they are driven to it by extreme necessity." He then declared, "Surely everything else ought to be tried before recourse is had to arms."[44] He probably was making reference here to a diplomatic solution to problems. This, in fact, is what he preferred. He preached, "An ambassador ought to be favored because he tends to maintain peace among men, or to remove troubles which have already started."[45]

Why did Calvin insist that the waging of war must be an option of last resort? There were two fundamental reasons that drove Calvin to embrace the last resort criterion as being part of the *jus ad bellum*. First, he feared war because of the difficulty entailed in bringing it to a conclusion, once it had begun. "Then let us conclude, that if warre bee once kindled, there is no remedy to appease it." In light of this sober fact, he gave this admonition: "And therefore it behooveth men to have the more staye of themselves beforehand."[46] In the second place, he was worried about the unintended effects that resulted even from a just war: "But wee must beare in minde, that although men bridle themselves as much as possible, yet there will bee too much evil committed." He went on to specify that war creates widows and fatherless children, and "though the goods and possessions

---

43. Bainton, *Christian Attitudes toward War and Peace*, 33, acknowledges that "the just war" is one in which there can only be "recourse to war as a very last resort after mediation had failed."

44. *Institutes* IV.20.12.

45. Sermon 30, *Sermons on 2 Samuel*, 451.

46. Sermon 118, *Sermons on Deuteronomy*, 726.

of men bee spared, yet are many men thrust out of their houses, and being ill handled die some for cold and some for want and penurie."[47] The contemplation of even a just war led Calvin to ask the rhetorical question: "Ought it not to bee a good bridle to us, when wee see so great enormities insue thereof?"[48]

Luther also regarded war as an option of last resort. He exhorted the European princes of his own day to "wait until the situation compels you to fight when you have no desire to do so." Even in this approach, he said, "You will still have more than enough wars to fight."[49] He also warned the political leaders of his generation about the consequences of not being committed to the principle of last resort: "It always happens and always has happened that those who begin war unnecessarily are beaten." He gave the reason for this by saying, "Ultimately, they cannot escape God's judgment and sword."[50]

While Calvin made repeated statements expressing a melancholy perspective about the perpetual wars that plague the human race, Luther took a more matter-of-fact approach. "War and killing," he wrote, "have been instituted by God." He meant—building upon the perspective of Romans 13—that "the sword has been instituted by God to punish evil, protect the good, and preserve peace." He recognized that because of what warfare achieves, it is a work that is "precious and godly." He urged the pacifists of his time that "they should also consider how great the plague is that war prevents." Luther elaborated upon what he meant by asking, "What are you going to do about the fact that people will not keep the peace, but rob, steal, kill, outrage women and children, and take away property and

47. Sermon 119, *Sermons on Deuteronomy*, 733.
48. Sermon 118, *Sermons on Deuteronomy*, 726.
49. *Whether Soldiers, Too, Can Be Saved*, 118.
50. Ibid.

honor?" He then declared, "The small lack of peace called war or the sword must set a limit to this universal, worldwide lack of peace which would destroy everyone."[51] Luther thus contended that there are but two alternatives. We may have total war by doing nothing—by abolishing the state, the soldier, and the sword. Or we may have limited war by using the same. Luther was quite pragmatic as to which option he would choose. His matter-of-fact stance is seen in his statement that "the office of soldier, or the sword" is "godly and as needful and useful to the world as eating and drinking or any other work."[52]

Warfare may be compared to a surgical procedure performed by a physician. "A good doctor sometimes finds so serious and terrible a sickness that he must amputate or destroy a hand, foot, eye, to save the body," said Luther. He added, "Looking at it from the point of view of the organ that he amputates, he appears to be a cruel and merciless man; but looking at it from the point of view of the body, which the doctor wants to save, he is a fine and true man and does a good and Christian work, as far as the work itself is concerned."[53] In the same way, the work of the soldier in "killing the wicked" appears "contrary to Christian love." But when one considers what the soldier is seeking to accomplish, one must take the opposite view. "When I think," Luther said, "of how it protects the good and keeps and preserves wife and child, house and farm, property, and honor and peace, then I see how precious and godly this work is."[54]

The metaphor of the surgeon and amputation was also used by Bullinger, but in a slightly different way. The radical nature of amputation, he argued, necessitated that it be a rem-

51. Ibid., 96
52. Ibid., 97.
53. Ibid., 96.
54. Ibid.

edy of last resort, as war likewise should be. "War is to commonweals a remedy indeed, but perilous and dangerous, even as lancing or cutting is to members." He elaborated, "The hand is poisoned . . . yet thou cuttest not off thy hand until, when thou hast tried all other medicines, thou dost plainly perceive that no other means can remedy the sore but cutting off alone." He then made his point: "Likewise, when all helps fail, then at the last let the war begin."[55] Since war, therefore, was viewed as a remedy by Bullinger, it had a good function. Nevertheless, because perils and dangers attend the remedy, he believed that it should only be used as a last resort.

Vermigli also showed familiarity with the human body metaphor. He affirmed that "warre is taken in hand for peace sake." He then declared, "And of this thing we may have a similitude of our owne bodies. For who would so live, as he should perpetuallie wrestle against diseases."[56] Warring, then, for the sake of peace is often necessary—in the same way that we must continually fight against disease in our own bodies. But warfare, although sometimes necessary, should be an act of last resort: "And although warre be just, yet must it not straightway bee taken in hande. All meanes must be attempted, rather than we shoulde come to battailes." Sounding like Bullinger, Vermigli reminded his readers: "For Phisitions doe not seare or cut, but when it seemeth that in a manner the whole bodie is put in hazard."[57]

Like Calvin, Vermigli cautioned about initiating warfare because it is not always easy to bring it to a conclusion: "Thou canst not in verie deede after thou hast once begun, appoint an ende when thou wilt."[58] He also, like Calvin, urged that war be

55. Sermon 9, *Decades*, 380.
56. *The Common Places* IV.17.21.
57. *The Common Places* IV.17.9.
58. Ibid.

initiated with due care because of all the evils which accompany it. Vermigli drew attention to quite a list of consequences that follow from war:

> All Religion vanisheth away, good lawes and customes are abolished, good manners are corrupted, artes are overwhelmed by oblivion, Cities and Townes are overthrown, the fieldes which were husbanded with great charges and labours, are destroyed, Treasures are forciblie taken away and unmeasurablie spent, men are slaine, or brought into servitude, women are defiled, or else enter in the yoke of bondage, or else have both evils done unto them.[59]

On the basis of such evils as these that follow war, Vermigli exhorted "even private men to praie unto God, that he will set over them such Princes, as be godly, wise, modest, and favourers of peace."[60]

We have seen from our discussion in this chapter that Calvin indeed embraced all of the elements that made up the *jus ad bellum* tradition. Previously we noted in chapters 2 and 4 that the justice of war in Calvin's thought required the proper civil authority to initiate warfare, either the prince or a parliamentary body. Here in Chapter 5, it has been demonstrated that Calvin developed his justice-of-war doctrine by including the other traditional constituents of just cause and right intention. He also added a stipulation regarding the necessity of last resort, preferring to resolve the dispute at hand through diplomacy.

---

59. *The Common Places* IV.17.22.
60. Ibid.

6

Political Legacy

Calvin taught a doctrine of two spheres. He therefore separated church and state with respect to their distinct jurisdictions, giving different roles to ministers and magistrates. It should also be recognized that he conceived of a symmetrical relationship between church and state as each sphere handled the responsibilities appointed to it by God.

Pastors were called by the Lord to wield the sword of the Spirit in the preaching of the Word; so likewise were princes summoned by God to unleash the sword of justice in the punishment of domestic evil and in battle against foreign powers. The principle of republicanism in the ecclesiastical realm, in which church officers were put into office by the suffrage of the people, was, in the best civil order possible, to be reflected in the elective principle of a republic. In each sphere, the people were to conduct themselves appropriately—the flock of God was to be in submission to their pastors and elders, and the citizens were to be in obedience to their governors. As ministers were to pastor the sheep committed to their charge, so politicians were to shepherd the flock of the commonwealth. The power of pastor and prince was not to be concentrated in each respective person. It was to be limited through the distribution of ecclesiastical power in a consistory and by placing political authority in a parliamentary body. A consistory or parliament would further check the power of pastor or prince by acting as a disciplinary body, if such a restraint should be needed.

The doctrine that Calvin set forth regarding church and state was fundamentally based upon his biblical exegesis. His conception of the pastor and his duties was largely based upon his study in the New Testament, while his understanding of the magistrate and his call mainly rested upon his exegetical work in the Old Testament.[1] He believed, nevertheless, that the holy war conduct of Moses, Joshua, and David was an historical, punitive act upon reprobate nations of antiquity, in which God used Israel as an instrument of divine wrath. For Calvin the holy war laws and historical narratives did not have a continuing significance for the modern state in terms of providing a model for prosecuting war. While his pastoral theology was more narrowly constructed out of the materials of the New Testament documents, his doctrine of the state was informed by the major political philosophers of the Western intellectual tradition.

A MEDIEVAL CAST

It is therefore no surprise that from the perspective of an American political philosophy, certain aspects of the thought of Calvin on the doctrine of the state appear to be strikingly medieval.[2] The Madisonian approach embodied in the First Amendment of the United States Constitution—"Congress shall make no

---

1. The importance of Calvin's work in the Old Testament must be appreciated. Oberman, "John Calvin: The Mystery of His Impact," 2, reflects upon Calvin's commentaries on the Old Testament: "Calvin's proficiency in Hebrew made him into the most outstanding among the Christian Hebraists of his day and indeed the only sixteenth-century Christian interpreter of the Hebrew Scripture who is still relevant as a resource for modern textual studies."

2. Larson, "A Champion of the Original American Republic," 258–70.

law respecting an establishment of religion, or prohibiting the free exercise thereof"—was sharply different from the medieval mindset embraced by Calvin and the other Reformed thinkers of his time.[3] Beza, for example, expressed a view that Calvin and the Reformed whole-heartedly embraced: political authority is to be used for the implementation of the First Table of the Law. Beza stated, "I declare that it is the principal duty of a most excellent and pious ruler that he should apply whatever means, authority and power has been granted him by God to this end entirely that God may be truly recognized among his subjects and may, being recognized, be worshipped and adored as the supreme king of all kings."[4] Practically speaking, this perspective meant that Calvin believed in the legitimacy of the state providing financial support for the church. He himself had initially

---

3. The Madisonian ideas embodied in the First Amendment also stood in opposition to much of the political thought and practice of eighteenth-century Europe. The medieval mindset—against which Madison articulated his doctrine of freedom of religion—was still going strong in Spain. Pfeffer, *Church, State, and Freedom* makes the point that the Spanish Inquisition established by Ferdinand and Isabella in 1480 continued to function until 1834. In fact, "as late as 1781 it caused heretics to be burned at the stake" (22). Indeed, "the Inquisition was still a reality in 1787 and the spirit of medieval intolerance was far from extinguished" (29). In addition, the idea of a state-supported church continued to dominate in Europe for generations to come. "The situation of church-state relations in Europe in 1787, when the representatives of the American States met in Philadelphia to lay the constitutional foundation for the new republic" is nicely put into perspective by Pfeffer. He writes that "no nation had yet adopted as the basis of its church-state relationship the principle of mutual independence of religion and political government." "The system of jurisdictionalism which prevailed all over Europe" meant that "one faith was favored as the official state-supported religion, but other faiths were permitted to exist with varying degrees of freedom" (Ibid.).

4. *Concerning the Rights of Rulers*, 82.

been retained by the government in Geneva to be a biblical teacher.[5]

No doubt Calvin recognized that the down-side of state financial support was state authority over church affairs. Perhaps the classic example of this with respect to Calvin related to his desire for weekly communion. The state, however, only permitted the sacrament of the Lord's Supper four times each year—on Easter, Pentecost, the first Sunday in September, and Christmas. The government, which paid Calvin's salary, dictated how the worship of God on this issue was to go.

Calvin nevertheless accepted an established church framework. He also embraced the idea of a holy commonwealth, which precluded any commitment to freedom of religion for groups that may have dissented from the prevailing orthodoxy. Since Calvin held to a territorial church model, all the inhabitants of the Geneva city-state necessarily belonged to the church, a church with a Reformed confession and liturgy.[6] People who desired the freedom to practice another religion had to go elsewhere to do so. This complete identification of church and state was the medieval ideal.[7]

The belief of Calvin that heresy was a crime that merited capital punishment was a very medieval conception.[8] Aquinas had articulated the same perspective in his assertion that heretics "have deserved not only to be separated from the Church, but to be eliminated from the world by death." His basic assumption here was that "it is a far graver matter to corrupt the faith which is the life of the soul than to falsify money which sustains the

---

5. McGrath, *A Life of John Calvin*, 96; Wallace, *Calvin, Geneva and the Reformation*, 16.

6. Rice and Grafton, *The Foundations of Early Modern Europe*, 167.

7. Bainton, *The Reformation of the Sixteenth Century*, 117–18.

8. *Commentaries on the Last Four Books of Moses*, 76.

temporal life." Aquinas then reasoned: "If it be just that forgers and other malefactors are put to death without mercy by the secular authority, with how much greater reason may heretics be not only excommunicated, but also put to death, when once they are convicted of heresy."[9]

Reasoning from the lesser to the greater, as Aquinas did, was a method of argumentation that was quite acceptable to Calvin. In his exposition of Zechariah 13:3, Calvin reasoned as follows: "For if at this day thieves and robbers and sorcerers are justly punished, doubtless those who as far as they can destroy souls . . . ought not to escape unpunished."[10] This perspective that the crime of heresy merited capital punishment was imbedded in the Justinian Code, which had been part of the civil law of Europe for one thousand years.[11] Medieval thinkers tended to regard the Justinian Code as a faithful reflection of natural law. This is seen in the thought of Salisbury. Mentioning Josiah the ancient king of Judah, Salisbury affirmed that it was the view of Josiah that the real glory of his kingship consisted in the fact that he subjected himself and his subjects to "the bonds of the divine law." He then drew attention to a Christian prince such as Justinian. Referring to the Justinian Code, Salisbury stated that Justinian disclosed and proclaimed "the most sacred laws," seeking "to consecrate the whole world as a temple of justice."[12]

On October 26, 1553, the Spanish heretic Michael Servetus was put to death by the civil magistrates of Geneva. Calvin had asked that Servetus be spared the agony of being burned to death, urging the Small Council to use the more

9. *Summa Theologica* 2a2ae, q. 11, art. 3. Quoted from *Aquinas: Selected Political Writings*, 79.

10. *Commentaries on the Prophet Zechariah*, 382.

11. Kelly, *The Emergence of Liberty in the Modern World*, 27.

12. *Policraticus* IV.6.

humane method of beheading. The government refused this request.[13] Calvin nevertheless concurred with this judgment of the state. He believed that the law of God demanded "capital punishment" for "the authors of apostasy, and so who pluck up religion by the roots."[14] He expressed his belief that the state must punish heretics within a Christian commonwealth. "In a well constituted polity," he affirmed, "profane men are by no means to be tolerated, by whom religion is subverted."[15] In this, Muller reminds us that Calvin was a man of his own time. "Even when his doctrinal statements appear at their most objective and apodictic they remain rooted in his time, determined by the materials he read."[16]

The execution of Servetus, though, must be kept in perspective. The Republic of Geneva was in fact highly restrained in comparison with the Kingdom of France. While Calvin argued that the capital crime of heresy ought not to be measured out "on account of some particular or trifling error," the situation in France was much different.[17] In the Catholic kingdom, the definition of heresy "broadened and deepened" to such an extent that it included the mere fact that a person had traveled to Geneva. A trip to Geneva became a capital crime.[18] In addition, the vast gap between Geneva and France is seen in terms of the number of heresy executions that occurred. This is reflected, for example, in a comparison between two cities, Geneva and Toulouse. During the ministry of Calvin, the Small Council executed one person for heretical teaching—Michael Servetus. He

13. Parker, *John Calvin*, 145.
14. *Commentaries on the Last Four Books of Moses*, 74–75.
15. Ibid., 75.
16. Muller, *The Unaccommodated Calvin*, 187.
17. *Commentaries on the Last Four Books of Moses*, 74–75.
18. Greengrass, *The French Reformation*, 34.

had denied the Christian dogma of the Trinity.[19] The *parlement* of Toulouse, conversely, sentenced sixty-two people to be burned at the stake.[20] We must keep in mind that the *parlement* of Toulouse was just one French court. People accused of heresy, many of whom were Protestants who did believe in the Trinity, were also condemned to die in the flames by other courts in France.

Finally, with respect to Calvin's medieval approach toward the problem of heresy, it must be realized that magisterial punishment of a heretic in a Christian society is distinct from magisterial prosecution of holy war.[21] The Reformed carefully distinguished between the judicial punishment of the state—"the magistrate . . . administering punishments"—directed against "all murderers" and "the impious"[22] and the taking up of arms by a government for the purpose of suppressing "the seditious stirrings of restless men" and protecting a commonwealth from attack by an enemy.[23] Calvin reflected this distinction in his thinking by carefully placing these two aspects of the authority of the state in different paragraphs in the *Institutes*—first dealing with the matter of judicial punishment in *Institutes* IV.20.10 and then treating the subject of warfare in *Institutes* IV.20.11–12.[24]

---

19. Attacks upon the Trinity continued to be regarded as a capital crime into the seventeenth century. The *Maryland Act Concerning Religion* (1649) is an example of this.

20. Greengrass, *The French Reformation*, 36.

21. Bainton missed this distinction when he maintained that Calvin believed in holy war on the basis of passages in which Calvin was merely affirming the duty of the state to punish heretics within the Christian commonwealth. See *Christian Attitudes toward War and Peace*, 145.

22. *Institutes* IV.20.10.

23. *Institutes* IV.20.11.

24. Bullinger made the same contrast between these two uses of the magistrate's sword in Sermon 9 of *Decades*.

In addition, he separated these two aspects of a government's use of the sword in this statement: "Therefore, both natural equity and the nature of the office dictate that princes must be armed not only to restrain the misdeeds of private individuals by judicial punishment, but also to defend by war the dominions entrusted to their safekeeping, if at any time they are under enemy attack."[25] Whereas a war could be legally prosecuted solely by the determination of a prince, impiety within a Christian nation and the punishment thereof was a matter that related to "capital punishment."[26] There had to be the involvement of judges, for "God commends the care and study of religion to the judges."[27] There had to be a "public trial."[28] There had to be the presentation of evidence, a "giving" of "testimony."[29] There had to be due process in which "a lawful examination shall have been previously instituted."[30]

On the idea of freedom of religion, Calvin reflected an essentially medieval mindset. On this issue, we are reminded that he belonged to a different time than we do. Some five hundred years have come and gone since the year of his birth. Yet, on the other hand, his teaching seems to stand at the beginning of the world in which we live. Calvin indeed bequeathed to us important conceptions, showing that he was remarkably influential in terms of his political doctrine.

---

25. *Institutes* IV.20.11.
26. *Commentaries on the Last Four Books of Moses*, 75.
27. Ibid., 73.
28. Ibid., 83.
29. Ibid., 84.
30. Ibid., 78.

PARLIAMENTARY WARFARE

The first highly influential element in Calvin's political philosophy was his teaching regarding war—both his discussion regarding the popular magistrates and their duty to rise up in defense of freedom against tyrannical government and his commitment to medieval just war theory. Unlike Luther and Bullinger, Calvin provided a parliamentary remedy for the perennial evil of tyranny. The *populares magistratus*, he taught, were "appointed to restrain the willfulness of kings."[31] Calvin here authorized the taking up of arms by a parliamentary body against a despotic government. With Vermigli and Beza siding with Calvin on this right, a body of Reformed thought was established to which succeeding generations could appeal for teaching, direction, and justification for taking up arms.

It seems quite evident that Calvin and the Reformed tradition on parliamentary resistance had a bearing in the American Revolution, labeled the Presbyterian Rebellion.[32] The magistrates of the people who had been sent to Philadelphia by the thirteen colonial governments formed a representative body in the Second Continental Congress. The point at issue, which resulted in the armed conflict—the raising of state militias and the Continental Army commanded by George Washington—was tyranny, the

31. *Institutes* IV.20.31.

32. There can be little doubt that the teaching of Calvin and the Reformed had a connection to the Dutch Rebellion against the Spanish King Philip II, who persecuted Protestants in the Netherlands. Reformed teaching on parliamentary resistance also would have impacted the English Civil War and the fact that the Puritans decided to go to war against the Cavaliers. This was the very thing that Calvin had in mind—armed resistance by a parliamentary body against an absolutist king, in this case, Charles I. Cf. Kingdon, "The First Expression of Theodore Beza's Political Ideas," 88; Clarke, *Our Southern Zion*, 91; Witte, *Religion and the American Constitutional Experiment*, 13.

trampling down of legal rights, either by King George III, Prime Minister Lord North, or the British Parliament as a whole.

Calvin's doctrine of the just war anticipated modern developments. Unlike the Zurich tradition in Bullinger and Vermigli on the issue of justice in war, which paved the way for holy war ideas and practice in the English Civil War, Calvin stood without wavering in the medieval just war tradition as it concerned both the justice of war and justice in war. He insisted that a war that pleased God had to meet the *jus ad bellum* criteria: legitimate authority, just cause, right intention, and last resort. In addition, when a state determined that a given war was morally justified, it also had to be concerned about godly warfare. A government, Calvin taught, had to give attention to the moral obligation of *jus in bello*.[33] He here affirmed the necessity of discrimination, or restraint and humanity toward noncombatants as well as to combatants who laid down their arms appealing for mercy. With respect to both of these issues, the justice of war and justice in war, he embraced positions that stand in continuity with modern just war theories.[34]

REPUBLICANISM IN GOVERNMENT

Calvin stood at the beginning of a new era. His political philosophy anticipated the modern epoch in his commitment to the superiority of a democratic-republic as a form of civil polity, rather than a monarchy.

---

33. It is interesting that in the American Revolutionary War, the so-called Presbyterian Rebellion, the engagements between the British and the Americans were characterized by a remarkable commitment to the ideas of justice in war, namely humanity and restraint. McDonald, "Eighteenth-Century Warfare as a Cultural Ritual," 39–58, expounds upon the rules of engagement and the civility that marked numerous Revolutionary War battles.

34. Kennedy, "Can War Be Justified?" 436–42.

Rule by kings and queens had been the government of choice through the Middle Ages.[35] Calvin, however, did not appreciate monarchy. On the basis of history and his own experience he exhibited a "sharp dislike of kingship."[36] Bouwsma puts his position in even stronger terms. "He shared the civic humanists' hatred of the Roman Empire for subverting the Republic."[37] What Calvin was particularly concerned about were "the encroachments of an emerging absolutism of his own day."[38] He wrote about "kings themselves, who seem unrestrained by laws."[39] He complained that "The world today is inundated with a flood of impiety and iniquity." He then specified, "We see so much plundering and robbery of people everywhere, and kings and princes thinking they deserve everything they want, simply because no one opposes them."[40]

What was particularly troublesome to constitutionalists like Calvin was that the sixteenth century witnessed a rise in the defenders of royal absolutism.[41] Beza, for example, made reference to those who maintain that "the king is not bound by the laws."[42] There are people, he said, "who so far exalt the authority of kings and supreme rulers as to dare maintain that they have

35. McDonald, *The Presidency of George Washington*, 1, reminds us that the government of choice for "nearly every other civilized country," even through the eighteenth century, was monarchy.

36. McNeill, "Calvin Preferred Representative Democracy," 30. Cf. Singer, *John Calvin*, 40.

37. Bouwsma, *John Calvin*, 208.

38. Singer, *John Calvin*, 42.

39. *Commentary on the Book of Psalms*, 22.

40. Sermon 29, *Sermons on 1 Samuel*, 67.

41. Kuyper, *Lectures on Calvinism*, 98–99, makes the point that it is against "State-omnipotence" and "the pride of absolutism" that "Calvinism protests."

42. *Concerning the Rights of Rulers*, 68.

no other Judge but God alone to whom they are bound to render account of their deeds."[43] There were those, contended Beza, who viewed the transformation of "the French monarchy into tyranny" as "the emancipation of the sovereign" or "his release from slavery."[44] Calvin opposed absolutism, recognizing that boundless and unlimited power inevitably leads to the abuse of that power. Thus he knew that absolutism had to be tamed. "It was clear to him that no European order would emerge unless royal absolutism were to be contained and harnessed by the rule of law."[45]

What was the solution to the perpetual tendency of monarchies to degenerate into tyranny?[46] The remedy in the view of Calvin was to be found in a republic.[47] He was without a doubt a "political republican."[48] He articulated his view with utter clarity, "A system compounded of aristocracy and democracy far excels all others."[49] His public preaching was no less clear. In Sermon 29 in his series through 1 Samuel, he affirmed, "For as Scripture teaches, a well-constituted republic is a singular benefit of God."[50] The advantage of a republic related to the issue of liberty. He stated, "I freely admit that no kind of government is

43. Ibid., 64.

44. Ibid., 61.

45. Oberman, "*Europa afflicta*," 107.

46. It should be noted that Calvin did not focus his attention solely upon tyranny as it found a nest within the locus of monarchical governments. In his *Commentaries on the Prophet Amos*, 269–70, he also expressed his concerns about tyranny finding a place of lodging within "the courts of justice." Tyranny could well involve judges who have "spared murderers" or perhaps have "deprived miserable men of their right."

47. Sap, *Paving the Way for Revolution*, 68–69.

48. McNeill, "Calvin Preferred Representative Democracy," 32.

49. *Institutes* IV.20.8.

50. Sermon 29, *Sermons on 1 Samuel*, 67.

more happy than one where freedom is regulated with coming moderation."⁵¹ It is clear from his biblical commentary work that he believed that the right to vote is a major constituent in what freedom actually entails: "In this especially consists the best condition of the people, when they can choose, by common consent, their own shepherds." He believed that the Lord in fact had given to Israel the best possible form of government: "The Lord . . . ordained among the Israelites an aristocracy bordering on democracy, since he willed to keep them in best condition until he should bring forward the image of Christ in David."⁵²

Here it must be stressed that Calvin was not advocating democracy as the solution for despotic governments.⁵³ It is quite clear that Calvin feared democracy above every form of civil polity.⁵⁴ He worried about its "deterioration into anarchy."⁵⁵ Like Aquinas, who stated his concern about sedition as being "a special sin" when "one part of the state rises in tumult against another part,"⁵⁶ Calvin articulated his fears regarding sedition: "The fall

51. *Institutes* IV.20.8.

52. Ibid.

53. Singer, *John Calvin*, 40.

54. Like Calvin, Bullinger expressed concern about a democracy as a form of government because of its tendency to degenerate into sedition. Bullinger in Sermon 6, the *Decades*, 311, put it this way: "And yet none can deny, but that great perils and infinite discommodities are in the aristocracy, but far more many in democracy." What was the great peril of democracy in the thinking of Bullinger? Democracy, technically speaking, he said, was a polity "wherein all the people together bear the whole sway and absolute authority" (Ibid., 310). This would then lead to what? Bullinger declared, "This kind of government breaketh out commonly into outrageous tumults. I mean, into seditions and conspiracies: for no man will suffer himself to be corrected, while every man will challenge to himself full and absolute authority to do what he lusteth."

55. McNeill, "Calvin Preferred Representative Democracy," 34.

56. *Summa Theologica* 2a2ae, q. 42, art. 1.

from kingdom to tyranny is easy; but it is not much more difficult to fall from the rule of the best men to the faction of the few; yet it is easiest of all to fall from popular rule to sedition."[57]

The trajectory from Calvin, specifically his advocacy of republicanism and his distaste for democracy, down to the American Constitutional Convention of 1787 is unmistakable.[58] James Madison and the other Framers feared democracy. At the same time, they not only wrote in favor of a republic, but they actually established one in the United States of America.[59] Republicanism, the principle of representative democracy, was the form of government enshrined in the Constitution.[60] In Number X of *The Federalist*, Madison wrote about the dangerous vice of faction in a society. The cure for the mischief of faction, he contended, is to be found in a republic rather than in a democracy. The danger of a pure democracy is that a majority faction will "sacrifice the weaker party." Appealing to the historical record regarding the longevity of democracies, Madison revealed his dread of this form of government: "Such democracies have ever been spectacles of turbulence and contention; have ever been found incompatible with personal security or the rights of property; and have in general been as short in their lives as they have been violent in their deaths."[61]

57. *Institutes* IV.20.8.

58. The Calvinian trajectory regarding democracy likewise reached seventeenth-century American Puritanism. John Cotton, the premier theologian in Massachusetts Bay, wrote, "Democracy, I do not conceive that God ever did ordain as a fit government either for church or for commonwealth. If the people be governors, who shall be governed?" Quoted in Singer, *A Theological Interpretation of American History*, 18.

59. Writing about the Constitution, Keillor, in *This Rebellious House*, 97, concludes, "It was brilliantly designed to curb democratic excess."

60. McDonald, *Novus Ordo Seclorum*, 67.

61. Madison, Number X, 126.

Just as Madison vigorously spoke against a democracy as a form of civil polity, he praised a republic—a form of government in which political wisdom would be found among a chosen elite. A central difference between a democracy and a republic, he stated is "the delegation of the government, in the latter to a small number of citizens elected by the rest." What consequence did Madison hope to achieve by this structure? "The effect" of this would be "to refine and enlarge the public views by passing them through the medium of a chosen body of citizens, whose wisdom may best discern the true interest of their country and whose patriotism and love of justice will be least likely to sacrifice it to temporary or partial considerations." Madison continued, "Under such a regulation it may well happen that the public voice, pronounced by the representatives of the people, will be more consonant to the public good than if pronounced by the people themselves, convened for the purpose."[62]

This statement shows that Madison would have rejected the egalitarian idea of a radical social and political equality between human beings, the idea that "every man is as good as his neighbor."[63] Indeed, there can be no question that the Constitutional Convention did not produce a document inspired by an egalitarian philosophy. The legitimacy of some kind of social stratification is assumed in the Constitutional provision regarding accession to office. Representatives alone were to be popularly elected (Art. I Sec. 2). Senators were to be chosen by the state legislatures (Art. I Sec. 3). The president was to be selected by electors (Art. II Sec. 1), and federal judges were to be appointed by the president (Art. II Sec. 2). Clearly, much of the nation's political authority came into power through the determination of different levels of privilege in the stratified social order. The

---

62. Ibid.
63. Bailey, *The American Pageant*, 256.

hierarchical arrangement of the new American Republic would have found a sixteenth-century advocate in Calvin. He stated, "It is necessary that they whom the Lord has advanced with peculiar gifts should be pre-eminent among others; and it is advantageous that there should be distinction of ranks in the world."[64]

There is a trajectory from Calvin down to Madison and the Founding Fathers. Their commitment to the principle of republicanism is patent.[65] But where more specifically is Calvin's political influence the most pronounced? It may well be the case that "it was in the formation of the Constitution of the United States in the Convention of 1787."[66]

As we examine this issue more carefully, we must appreciate the fact that Calvin's republican principles were reflected both in his doctrine of the church and in his doctrine of the state. Genevan Presbyterianism was neither monarchical (Episcopalian) nor democratic (Congregational). It was an ecclesiastical republic. Although the ministers determined which man would become a pastoral candidate, the approved candidate was still required, according to the church constitution, to preach to the people in order that he may be accepted by the common consent of the faithful.[67] Calvin believed that biblical church government made

---

64. *Commentaries on the First Book of Moses Called Genesis*, 246.

65. Hudson, "Calvin a Source of Resistance Theory, and Therefore of Democracy," 22, reflects upon the trajectory from Calvin down to Jefferson and Adams: "Even the term 'democratic republican,' which Jefferson adopted as his party label, was an affirmation of the 'mixed state' ideal. John Adams, who certainly ought to have known what was in the minds of the early leaders, explicitly acknowledged the debt which the 'founding fathers' owed to Calvin and the political theorists of Calvinism."

66. Singer, *John Calvin*, 42.

67. *Ordonnances Ecclésiastiques*, 2.

provision for the suffrage of the people.[68] This fact surfaces not only in the *Ecclesiastical Ordinances*, but also in his biblical commentary on Acts 14:23. He pointed out that Paul and Barnabas did not appoint elders in the churches apart from the vote of the people. "Rather they suffer the matter to be decided by the consent of them all," wrote Calvin. What role did Paul and Barnabas actually have in the election of elders in the churches that they planted on their first missionary journey? Calvin answered, "In ordaining pastors the people had their free election, but lest there should any tumult arise, Paul and Barnabas sit as chief moderators."[69] As we have already seen, Calvin stood behind the same right of franchise in the institution of the state. The best arrangement, he affirmed, is when the people "can choose, by common consent, their own shepherds."[70]

In the teaching of Calvin, a symmetrical arrangement was to be found in ecclesiastical and civil government. There is a "close parallel between Calvin's conceptions of church polity and of the structure of political government."[71] In terms of Calvin's followers in the area of church polity, we find that the embrace of ecclesiastical republicanism prepared them to embrace the same republican ideal in the sphere of civil polity.[72] What has the appearance of Calvinism meant for the nations into which its doctrines have spread? "It has brought with it an almost irresistible urge to create a government which would be patterned after that of the Reformed and Presbyterian churches."[73] A good

68. Strohl, "Ministry in the Middle Ages and the Reformation," 41.

69. *Commentary on the Acts of the Apostles*, 27–28.

70. *Commentaries on the Prophet Micah*, 309–10.

71. McNeill, "Calvin Preferred Representative Government," 34.

72. Reid, "The Transmission of Calvinism in the Sixteenth Century," 77.

73. Singer, *John Calvin*, 42.

example of this is found early in the seventeenth century with the Stuart monarchy. James I of England well understood that "in the Puritan movement" there was "a real threat to his divine right theory of government."[74]

As we consider the ecclesiastical scene in America at the time of the Constitutional Convention, we must remember that despite the presence of Deism and agnosticism in figures like Thomas Paine and Ethan Allen, there continued to be a strong Reformed, even Presbyterian, element in the country. At the time of the Declaration of Independence in 1776, the population numbered approximately three million people. It has been estimated that perhaps as many as two out of three people came from a Reformed background.[75] There was indeed a significant Presbyterian influence in the population. At the time of the Revolutionary War, there were about half a million Scotch-Irish in America. This was one-sixth of the entire population.[76] It seems quite likely that ecclesiastical republicanism, alive and well in American Presbyterianism, spilled out into the civil arena. With respect to the Constitution of 1787, "It is no accident that the birth of the Republic coincided with the appearance of the national Presbyterian Church."[77]

We see then that Calvin cast a long shadow in America in terms of his legacy in political ethics. Monarchical tyranny, in his teaching, was an evil for which a remedy existed in representative political bodies—what he referred to as the magistrates of the people. Wars initiated by such parliamentary bodies were ethical and legal, but they had to be prosecuted in harmony with the tenets of justice-in-war teaching. A more fundamental

74. Ibid.
75. Kelly, *The Emergence of Liberty in the Modern World*, 120.
76. Thompson, *Presbyterians in the South*, 1:43.
77. Singer, *John Calvin*, 43.

antidote to tyranny was to be found, however, in a republican form of government. Freedom would be better protected in a civil polity in which the people had the right to choose their own political leaders. The resistance of the Second Continental Congress to British tyranny in 1776 and the establishment of republican principles in the Constitution of the United States of America in 1787 owe much to the political thought of John Calvin.

Conclusion

REFORMED POLITICAL thought has moved past the disregard for liberty of conscience that Calvin manifested in continuity with the medieval mindset. The Reformed now have a vision for a society that is not only virtuous, but also free. There is now the recognition reflected in a theologian like Abraham Kuyper that freedom in a social order is a singular benefit from the Heavenly Father, "a *gift* from God."[1] It was Kuyper who stated that "the primordial and inalienable right of all men" is "liberty of conscience" for "each and every citizen," which necessarily includes "*liberty of speech*" and "*liberty of worship*."[2]

There is no question, nevertheless, that the overall Calvin legacy on the state and war provides legitimacy to the perspective that "Calvin emerges as the brightest star in a galaxy of Reformed theologians."[3] It was Calvin and his doctrine of armed resistance by a parliamentary body that provided theological and moral legitimacy among the Reformed for the suppression of tyranny in the American Revolution—a matter concerning which Bullinger remained silent, never providing an institutional remedy for the problem of tyranny. It was Calvin, rather than Bullinger or Vermigli, who ever insisted upon restraint and humanity in war. He thus closed the door to the possibility of a

---

1. Kuyper, "Freedom," 319.

2. Kuyper, *Lectures on Calvinism*, 108.

3. Donnelly, "Italian Influences on the Development of Calvinist Scholasticism," 81. Cf. Thompson, *Humanists and Reformers*, 471; Leith, *Introduction to the Reformed Faith*, 127.

widespread embrace of holy war doctrine among the Reformed. Indeed, it was Calvin and the church in Geneva that cast the long shadow of Presbyterian ecclesiastical polity down to the present time, rather than the Erastian structure developed by Bullinger.[4] This meant that Reformed churches for the most part would have the freedom to be led by their own officers elected by the congregation, rather than being governed by the civil magistrates.[5] The presence of ecclesiastical republicanism

4. It is instructive to note Calvin's own assessment of what he had achieved in the establishment of the Geneva consistory. Soon after the consistory began its meetings near the end of 1541, Calvin wrote a letter to his friend Oswald Myconius (on March 14, 1542), in which he reflected upon his successful effort to establish the Geneva consistory: "We at length possess a Presbyterial Court, such as it is, and a form of discipline, such as these disjointed times permit" (*Letters of John Calvin*, 1:316). This expression "Nunc habemus qualecunque presbyterorum judicium" is most significant (*Calvini Opera*, vol. 11, 379). Calvin believed that he had established a church government that should be regarded as presbyterian. The essential elements of Calvin's rudimentary presbyterian structure—which later would appear in the fully developed Presbyterianism emanating from the Westminster Assembly—were these: all the pastors were equal (without a superior bishop over them); pastors and elders shared together in the government of the church (rather than being under the dominance of the civil magistrate alone); and the consistory, composed of pastors and elders, had ecclesiastical authority over the multiple congregations in the Geneva Republic. Several scholars recognize that the roots of Presbyterianism go back to sixteenth-century Geneva. See Loetscher, *A Brief History of the Presbyterians*, 23; Kingdon, "Calvin and 'Presbytery': the Geneva Company of Pastors," 43–55; Coertzen, "Presbyterial Church Government: Ius Divinum, Ius Ecclesiasticum or Ius Humanum?" 340; Baker, "Church, State, and Toleration," 528.

5. Baker, "Erastianism in England," 328, states, "By the 1550s, there were two approaches: the doctrine of the single sphere in Zurich and the two kingdoms theory in Geneva. Soon the disagreement spread from the Swiss cities into the Palatinate, France, the Netherlands, Scotland,

within countries in which Presbyterianism found a home would provide a powerful impetus toward the creation of republican institutions in civil government. From the perspective of Calvin nothing could be better with respect to life in this world than for a people to have liberty, the right to choose their own political leaders.[6] Among the Reformed in the sixteenth century, it may be concluded that Calvin had the greatest long-range impact in terms of his political thought and its continued viability in the modern state.

---

and England. By the late sixteenth century, the two kingdoms theory of Calvinism had won victories in most of the Reformed churches—in France, Germany, the Netherlands, and Scotland."

6. The right of the people to choose their own leaders has implications with regard to the issue of the source of law in a society. The seventeenth-century Scottish Presbyterian Samuel Rutherford, *The Law and the Prince*, 114, referred to "the people" as being "the fountain of laws." George Buchanan, a major Reformed leader of the Church of Scotland in the sixteenth century, had the same perspective. In *The Rights of the Crown in Scotland*, 269, Buchanan stated that "God has ordered" the magistrates "to be conservators" of the law. The laws that would be so maintained, however, came from the people. "The people is the parent, or at least the author of the law, and has the power of its enactment or repeal at pleasure" (276). Calvin, of course, maintained that all human law should be in harmony with natural law. He recognized that far too much law is "abhorrent not only to all justice, but also to all humanity and gentleness." How did Calvin regard laws that are contrary to natural law, "that perpetual rule of love?" "I do not think that those barbarous and savage laws," he said, "are to be regarded as laws" (*Institutes* IV.20.15).

Bibliography

Primary Sources

Althusius, Johannes. *Politica*. Translated by Frederick S. Carney. Indianapolis: Liberty Fund, 1995.

Aquinas, Thomas. *Aquinas: Selected Political Writings*. Translated by J.W. Dawson. Oxford: Basil Blackwell, 1959.

———. *On Kingship, to the King of Cyprus*. Translated by Gerald B. Phelan. Toronto: Pontifical Institute of Mediaeval Studies, 1982.

———. *Summa Theologiae*. London and New York: Blackfriars, 1964–81.

———. *Summa Theologica*. 5 vols. New York: Benziger Brothers, 1948. Reprint, Allen, TX: Christian Classics, 1948.

Augustine. *Contra Faustum Manichaeum*. Corpus Scriptorum Ecclesiasticorum. Prague: F. Tempsky, 1881.

———. *Reply to Faustus the Manichaean*. Nicene and Post-Nicene Fathers. Edinburgh: T & T Clark; Grand Rapids: Eerdmans, 1996.

Bettenson, Henry, ed. *Documents of the Christian Church*. 2nd ed. London, Oxford, and New York: Oxford, 1963.

Beza, Theodore. *Concerning the Rights of Rulers over Their Subjects and the Duty of Subjects toward Their Rulers*. Translated by Henri-Louis Gonin. Capetown and Pretoria: H.A.U.M., 1956.

———. *De jure magistratuum*. Edited by Klaus Sturm. Neukirchen-Vluyn: Neukirchener Verlag, 1965.

———. *Du droit des magistrates*. Edited by Robert M. Kingdon. Geneva: Droz, 1970.

———. *The Life of John Calvin*. Translated by Henry Beveridge. Philadelphia: Westminster, 1909.

Buchanan, George. *The Rights of the Crown in Scotland*. Harrisonburg, VA: Sprinkle, 1982.

Bullinger, Henry. *Cinq Decades Qui Sont Cinquante Sermons*. Geneva: Michel Blanchier, 1574.

———. *Common Places of Christian Religion.* Translated by John Stockwood. London: Tho. East and H. Middleton, 1572.

———. *Confutation of the Popes Bull.* Translated by Arthur Golding. London: John Day, 1572.

———. *The Decades of Henry Bullinger.* Translated by H.I. Cambridge: University Press, 1849. Reprint, New York: Johnson, 1968.

———. *A Hundred Sermons upon the Apocalipse of Jesus Christ.* Translated by John Daus. London: John Daye, 1573.

———. *Sermonum Decades Quinque, De Potissimis Christianae Religionis Capitibus.* London: Excudebat Henricus Midletonus, 1587.

Calvin, John. *Calvin's Commentaries.* 54 vols. Edinburgh: Calvin Translation Society, 1843–55. Reprint, Grand Rapids: Baker Book House, 1979.

———. *Ecclesiastical Ordinances.* In *The Register of the Company of Pastors of Geneva in the Time of Calvin.* Translated by Philip E. Hughes. Grand Rapids: Eerdmans, 1966.

———. *Institutes of the Christian Religion.* 1536 Edition. Translated by Ford Lewis Battles. Grand Rapids: Eerdmans, 1986.

———. *Institutes of the Christian Religion.* 1559 Edition. Translated by Henry Beveridge. Grand Rapids: Eerdmans, 1989.

———. *Institutes of the Christian Religion.* 1559 Edition. Translated by Ford Lewis Battles. Philadelphia: Westminster, 1960.

———. *Ioannis Calvini Opera.* Corpus Reformatorum. Brunswick: C.A. Schwetzke, 1863–1900.

———. *John Calvin's Sermons on the Ten Commandments.* Translated by Benjamin W. Farley. Grand Rapids: Baker, 1980.

———. *Letters of John Calvin.* 4 vols. Translated by Jules Bonnet. New York: Lenox Hill, 1972.

———. *The Necessity of Reforming the Church.* Tracts and Treatises. Grand Rapids: Eerdmans, 1958.

———. *Ordonnances Ecclésiastiques.* In *Registres de la Compagnie des Pasteurs de Genève au temps de Calvin.* Geneva: Droz, 1964.

———. Sermon 29. *Sermons on 1 Samuel.* Translated by Douglas F. Kelly. In *Calvin Studies Colloquium.* Davidson, NC: Colloquium on Calvin Studies, 1982.

———. *Sermons on Deuteronomy.* Translated by Arthur Golding. London: Henry Middleton, 1583. Reprint, Edinburgh: Banner of Truth, 1987.

———. *Sermons on 2 Samuel.* Translated by Douglas F. Kelly. Edinburgh: Banner of Truth, 1992.

Carroll, Harry J. Jr., et al, eds. *The Development of Civilization.* Rev. ed. Glen View, IL: Scott, 1969.

Cicero, Marcus Tullius. *On Duties.* Cambridge Texts in the History of Political Thought. Cambridge: Cambridge, 1991.

Franklin, Julian H., ed. *Constitutionalism and Resistance in the Sixteenth Century: Three Treatises by Hotman, Beza, and Mornay.* New York: Pegasus, 1969.

Gouge, William. *Gods Three Arrowes.* London: George Miller, 1631.

Isidore of Seville. *Etymologiarum sive Originum Libri XX.* Oxford, 1911.

John of Salisbury. *Policraticus.* Translated by John Dickinson. New York: Alfred A. Knopf, 1927.

———. *Policraticus.* Abridged. New York: Frederick Unger, 1979.

Knox, John. *The Works of John Knox.* 6 vols. Edinburgh: Wodrow Society, 1864.

Luther, Martin. *Against the Robbing and Murdering Hordes of Peasants.* In *Luther's Works,* 46:45–56. St. Louis: Concordia; Philadelphia: Fortress, 1967.

———. *D. Martin Luthers Werke.* Weimar: Hermann Böhlaus Nachfolger, 1883–1987.

———. *Luther and Calvin on Secular Authority.* Cambridge Texts in the History of Political Thought. Cambridge: Cambridge, 1991.

———. *On War against the Turk.* In *Luther's Works,* 46:155–205. St. Louis: Concordia; Philadelphia: Fortress, 1967.

———. *Warning to His Dear German People.* In *Luther's Works,* 47: 3–55. Philadelphia: Fortress, 1971.

———. *Whether Soldiers, Too, Can Be Saved.* In *Luther's Works,* 46: 87–137. St. Louis: Concordia; Philadelphia: Fortress, 1967.

Madison, James. Number X. *The Federalist Papers.* London: Penguin Books, 1987.

Registers of the Consistory of Geneva in the Time of Calvin, vol. 1:1542–1544. Grand Rapids and Cambridge: Eerdmans, 2000.

Registres du Consistoire de Genève au Temps de Calvin, vol. 2:1545–1546. Geneva: Droz, 2001.

Registres du Consistoire de Genève au Temps de Calvin, vol. 3:1547–1548. Geneva: Droz, 2004.

Rutherford, Samuel. *The Law and the Prince.* Harrisonburg, VA: Sprinkle, 1982.

Vermigli, Peter Martyr. *The Common Places.* Translated by Anthony Marten. London, 1583.

———. *Loci Communes.* Edited by Robert Masson. London: Thomas Vautrollerius, 1583.

———. *The Political Thought of Peter Martyr Vermigli: Selected Texts and Commentary.* Edited by Robert M. Kingdon. Geneva: Droz, 1980.

Secondary Sources

Allen, John W. *A History of Political Thought in the Sixteenth Century.* 3rd ed. London: Methuen, 1951.

Anderson, Marvin W. "Peter Martyr, Reformed Theologian (1542–1562): His Letters to Heinrich Bullinger and John Calvin." *SCJ* 4 (1973) 41–64.

———. "Royal Idolatry: Peter Martyr and the Reformed Tradition." *ARH* 69 (1978) 157–201.

Anderson, Matthew S. *The Origins of the Modern European State System.* London and New York: Longman, 1998.

Armstrong, Brian G. *Calvinism and the Amyraut Heresy.* Madison, Milwaukee and London: University of Wisconsin Press, 1969.

———. "The Changing Face of French Protestantism: the Influence of Pierre Du Moulin." In *Calviniana: Ideas and Influence of Jean Calvin,* edited by Robert V. Schnucker, 131–49. Kirksville, MO: Sixteenth Century Journal, 1988.

———. "*Duplex cognitio Dei,* Or? The Problem and Relation of Structure, Form, Purpose in Calvin's Theology." In *Probing the Reformed Tradition,* edited by Elsie McKee et al, 135–53. Louisville: Westminster/John Knox, 1989.

———. "Exegetical and Theological Principles in Calvin's Preaching, with Special Attention to His Sermons on the Psalms." In *Ordenlich und Fruchtbar,* edited by Wilhelm H. Neuser et al, 191–209. Leiden: J. J. Groen En Zoon, 1997.

———. "The Nature and Structure of Calvin's Thought According to the *Institutes*: Another Look." In *John Calvin's Institutes: His Opus Magnum,* 55–81. Potchefstroom: Wetenskaplike Bydraes, 1986.

———. "The Nature of French Protestantism." In *Calvin—France— South Africa,* edited by Adrianus Drost Pont, 25–40. Pretoria: Kital, 1990.

———. "The Pastoral Office in Calvin and Pierre du Moulin." In *Calvin: Erbe und Auftrag*, edited by Willem Van't Spijker. Kampen: Kok Pharos, 1991.

———. "Report on the Seminar: An Investigation of Calvin's Principles of Biblical Interpretation." *Hervormde Teologiese* 54 (1998) 133–42.

———. "Response to 'Calvin's Conversion to Teachableness.'" In *Calvin and Christian Ethics*, edited by Peter De Klerk, 79–82. Grand Rapids: Calvin Studies Society, 1987.

———. "The Role of the Holy Spirit in Calvin's Teaching on the Ministry." In *Calvin and the Holy Spirit*, edited by Peter De Klerk, 99–111. Grand Rapids: Calvin Studies Society, 1989.

Arnold, Thomas F. *Renaissance at War*. London: Cassell, 2001.

Bailey, Thomas A. *The American Pageant: A History of the Republic*. 3rd ed. Boston: D.C. Heath, 1966.

Bainton, Roland H. *Christian Attitudes toward War and Peace: A Historical Survey and Critical Re-evaluation*. New York and Nashville: Abingdon, 1960.

———. "Congregationalism and the Puritan Revolution from the Just War to the Crusade." In *Studies in the Reformation*, edited by Roland H. Bainton, 248–74. Boston: Beacon, 1963.

———. *The Reformation of the Sixteenth Century*. Boston: Beacon, 1952.

Baird, Henry M. *Theodore Beza: The Counsellor of the French Reformation*. New York and London: G. P. Putnam's Sons, 1899.

Baker, J. Wayne. "Church, State, and Toleration: John Locke and Calvin's Heirs in England, 1644–1689." In *Later Calvinism: International Perspectives*, edited by W. Fred Graham, 525–43. Kirksville, MO: Sixteenth Century Journal, 1994.

———. "Covenant and Community in the Thought of Heinrich Bullinger." In *The Covenant Connection: From Federal Theology to Modern Federalism*, edited by Daniel J. Elazar et al, 15–29. Lanham, MD: Lexington, 2000.

———. "In Defense of Magisterial Discipline: Bullinger's 'Tractatus De Excommunicatione' of 1568." In *Heinrich Bullinger: 1504–1575*, edited by Ulrich Gäbler et al, 191–207. Zurich: Theologischer Verlag, 1975.

———. "Erastianism in England: The Zürich Connection." In *Die Zürcher Reformation: Ausstrahlungen und Rückwirkungen*, edited by Alfred Schlindler and Hans Stickelberger, 327–49. Bern: Peter Lang, 2001.

———. "Faces of Federalism: From Bullinger to Jefferson." *Publius* 30 (2000) 25–41.

———. *Heinrich Bullinger and the Covenant: The Other Reformed Tradition.* Athens, OH: Ohio University, 1980.

———. "Heinrich Bullinger, the Covenant, and the Reformed Tradition in Retrospect." *SCJ* 29 (1998) 359–76.

———. "John Owen, John Locke, and Calvin's Heirs in England." In *Calvin and the State*, edited by Peter De Klerk, 83–102. Grand Rapids: Calvin Studies Society, 1993.

Ball, Milner S. "The Significance for Political Theory and Action of Calvin's Sermons Second Samuel." In *Calvin Studies I*, edited by John H. Leith et al, 40–51. Davidson, NC: Davidson College, 1982.

Barilier, Roger. "Ordination Pastorale et Autorite du Ministere." *LRR* 41 (1990) 13–28.

Barnes, Jonathan. "The Just War." In *The Cambridge History of Later Medieval Philosophy*, edited by Norman Kretzman et al., 772–84. Cambridge: Cambridge, 1982.

Baron, Hans. "Was Calvin's Thought the Inspiration for the Earliest Democratic Revolts in Europe?" In *Calvin and Calvinism*, edited by Robert M. Kingdon et al, 50–55. Lexington, MA: D.C. Heath, 1970.

Baumgartner, Frederick J. *France in the Sixteenth Century.* New York: St. Martin's, 1995.

———. *Henry II: King of France, 1547–1559.* Durham and London: Duke University, 1988.

———. *Radical Reactionaries: The Political Thought of the French Catholic League.* Geneva: Droz, 1975.

Benoît, Jean-Daniel. *Calvin, Directeur d'ames: Contribution a l'histoire de la Piete.* Strasbourg: Editions Oberlin, 1947.

———. "Pastoral Care of the Prophet." In *John Calvin, Contemporary Prophet: A Symposium,* edited by Jacob T. Hoogstra, 51–67. Grand Rapids: Baker, 1959.

Bense, Walter F. "Calvinism and War." In *The Fall of Christianity*, edited by Gerrit Jan Heering, 14–18. New York and London: Garland, 1972.

Biel, Pamela. *Doorkeepers at the House of Righteousness: Heinrich Bullinger and the Zurich Clergy.* Bern: Peter Lang, 1991.

———. "Heinrich Bullinger and the Office of Minister: The Reformed Clergy in Zürich, 1535–1575." PhD diss., Columbia University, 1988.

Biéler, André. "La Pensée économique et sociale de Calvin." In *Protestantisme et Capitalisme,* edited by Philippe Besnard, 285–92. Paris: Librairie Armand Colin, 1970.

———. *L'umanesimo Sociale di Calvino.* Geneva: Labor et Fides, 1961.

Birmelé, André. "Le Ministere dans les Eglises de la Reforme." *PL* 29 (1981) 190–206.

Boeke, Brandt B. "Calvin's Doctrine of Civil Government." *SBT* 11 (1981) 57–79.

Bonivard, François de. "On the Ecclesiastical Polity of Geneva." In *Transition and Revolution,* edited by Robert M. Kingdon, 104–7. Minneapolis: Burges, 1974.

Bouwsma, William J. *John Calvin: A Sixteenth-Century Portrait.* New York: Oxford, 1988.

———. "The Peculiarity of the Reformation in Geneva." In *Religion and Culture in the Renaissance and Reformation,* edited by Steven Ozment. Kirksville, MO: Sixteenth Century Journal, 1989.

Bush, Eberhard. "Church and Politics in the Reformed Tradition." In *Major Themes in the Reformed Tradition,* edited by Donald K. McKim, 180–195. Grand Rapids: Eerdmans, 1992.

Cahier-Buccelli, G. "Dans l'ombre de la Réforme: les members de l'ancien clergédemeurés à Genève (1536–1558)." *BSJAG* 18 (1989) 367–89.

Cahill, Lisa Sowle. *Love Your Enemies: Discipleship, Pacifism, and Just War Theory.* Minneapolis: Fortress Press, 1994.

———. "Nonresistance, Defense, Violence, and the Kingdom in Christian Tradition." *Interpretation* 38 (1984) 380–97.

Cairns, Earle E. *Christianity through the Centuries.* Rev. ed. Grand Rapids: Zondervan, 1967.

Cartier, Alfred. "Les Idées Politiques de Théodore de Bèze d'après le Traité Du Droit des Magistrats sur leurs sujets." *BSHAG* 2 (1900): 41–56.

Chadwick, Owen. *The Reformation.* New York: Penguin, 1972.

Chenevière, Marc. "Did Calvin Advocate Theocracy?" *EQ* 9 (1937): 160–68.

Clarke, Erskine. *Our Southern Zion: A History of Calvinism in the South Carolina Low Country, 1690–1990.* Tuscaloosa and London: University of Alabama, 1996.

Coertzen, Peter. "Presbyterial Church Government: Ius Divinum, Ius Ecclesiasticum or Ius Humanum?" In *Calvin: Erbe und Auftrag,* edited by Willem van't Spijker, 329–42. Leuven: Peeters, 1991.

Collinson, Patrick. *The Reformation.* London: Weidenfeld and Nicholson, 2003.

Cottret, Bernard. *Calvin: A Biography*. Translated by M. Wallace McDonald. Grand Rapids: Eerdmans; Edinburgh: T. & T. Clark, 2000.

Davis, Paul K. *Encyclopedia of Invasions and Conquests: From Ancient Times to the Present*. New York and London: Norton, 1996.

Deane, Herbert A. *The Political and Social Ideas of St. Augustine*. New York and London: Columbia University, 1963.

De Boer, Erik A. "The Presence and Participation of Laypeople in the *Congrégations* of the Company of Pastors in Geneva." *SCJ* 35 (2004) 651–70.

De Ridder, Richard R. "John Calvin's Views on Discipline: A Comparison of the *Institution* of 1536 and the *Institutes* of 1559." *CTJ* 21 (1986) 223–30.

Dickens, Arthur G. *Reformation and Society in Sixteenth-Century Europe*. New York: Harcourt, 1966.

Donnelly, John Patrick. "Calvinist Thomism." *Viator* (1976) 441–55.

———. "Italian Influences on the Development of Calvinist Scholasticism." *SCJ* 7 (1976) 81–101.

———. "Peter Martyr Vermigli's Political Ethics." In *Peter Martyr Vermigli: Humanism, Republicanism, Reformation,* edited by Emidio Campi, 59–66. Geneva: Droz, 2002.

———. "The Social and Ethical Thought of Peter Martyr Vermigli." In *Peter Martyr Vermigli and Italian Reform,* edited by Joseph C McClelland, 107–119. Waterloo, ONT: Wilfrid Laurier University, 1980.

Doumergue, Emile. *Calvin Le Fondateur de Libertés Modernes*. Montauban: J. Granié, 1898.

Dowey, Edward A. "Calvin on Church and State." *RPW* 24 (1957) 244–52.

———. "Heinrich Bullinger as Theologian: Thematic, Comprehensive, Schematic." In *Calvin Studies V*, edited by John H. Leith, 41–60. Davidson, NC: Calvin Colloquium, 1990.

———. "The Word of God as Scripture and Preaching." In *Later Calvinism: International Perspectives*, edited by W. Fred Graham, 5–18. Kirksville, MO: Sixteenth Century Journal, 1994.

Dunn, Richard S. *The Age of Religious Wars, 1559–1689*. New York: Norton, 1970.

Elwood, Christopher. *The Body Broken: The Calvinist Doctrine of the Eucharist and the Symbolization of Power in Sixteenth-Century France*. New York and Oxford: Oxford, 1999.

Engammare, Max. "Calvin monarchomaque? Du soupcon à l'argument." *ARH* 89 (1998) 207–26.

Forrester, Duncan B. "Martin Luther and John Calvin." In *History of Political Philosophy*, edited by Leo Strauss et al, 277–313. Chicago: Rand McNally, 1963.

Foster, Herbert D. "Calvin and His Followers Championed Representative Government." In *Calvin and Calvinism*, edited by Robert M. Kingdon et al, 36–45. Lexington, MA: D.C. Heath, 1970.

Gamble, Richard C. "*Brevitas et facilitas:* Toward an Understanding of Calvin's Hermeneutic." *WTJ* 47 (1985) 1–17.

———. "The Christian and the Tyrant: Beza and Knox on Political Resistance Theory." *WTJ* 46 (1984) 125–39.

Ganoczy, Alexandre. "Calvin." In *The Reformation*, edited by Pierre Chaunu, 120–36. New York: St. Martin's, 1990.

———. *The Young Calvin.* Translated by David Foxgrover and Wade Provo. Philadelphia: Westminster, 1987.

Garrison, Janine. *A History of Sixteenth Century France, 1493–1598.* Translated by Richard Rex. New York: St. Martin's, 1995.

Gatis, G. Joseph. "The Political Theory of John Calvin." *BS* 153 (1996) 449–67.

George, Timothy. "War and Peace in the Puritan Tradition." *CH* 53 (1984) 492–503.

Giesey, Ralph E. "The Monarchomach Triumvirs: Hotman, Beza and Mornay." *BHR* 32 (1970) 41–56.

Gill, Robin. *A Textbook of Christian Ethics.* Edinburgh: T. & T. Clark, 1985.

Godfrey, W. Robert. "Calvin and Theonomy." In *Theonomy: A Reformed Critique*, edited by William S. Barker et al, 298–312. Grand Rapids: Zondervan, 1990.

Gosselin, Edward A. "David in *Tempore Belli:* Beza's David in the Service of the Huguenots." *SCJ* 7 (1976) 31–54.

Graham, W. Fred. "Calvin and the Political Order: An Analysis of the Three Explanatory Studies." In *Calviniana: Ideas and Influence of Jean Calvin*, edited by Robert V. Schnucker, 51–61. Kirksville, MO: Sixteenth Century Journal, 1988.

———. *The Constructive Revolutionary: John Calvin and His Socio-Economic Impact.* Richmond: John Knox, 1971.

Greaves, Richard L. "Calvinism, Democracy, and the Political Thought of John Knox." In *Occasional Papers of the American Society for*

Reformation Research, edited by Robert Cutler, 81–92. St. Louis: American Society for Reformation Research, 1977.

———. *Theology and Revolution in the Scottish Reformation: Studies in the Thought of John Knox.* Grand Rapids: Eerdmans, 1980.

Greef, Wulfert de. *The Writings of John Calvin: An Introductory Guide.* Translated by Lyle D. Bierma. Grand Rapids: Baker, 1993.

Greengrass, Mark. *The French Reformation.* Oxford: Basil Blackwell, 1987.

Grimm, Harold J. *The Reformation Era, 1500–1650.* 2nd ed. New York: Macmillan; London: Collier-Macmillan, 1973.

Grin, Edmond. "Calvin Pasteur." *RTP* (1949) 202–5.

Haller, William. *The Rise of Puritanism.* Philadelphia: University of Pennsylvania, 1984.

Hallowell, John H. *Main Currents in Modern Political Thought.* New York: Holt, Rinehart and Winston, 1950.

Hancock, Ralph C. *Calvin and the Foundations of Modern Politics.* Ithaca and London: Cornell, 1989.

———. "Religion and the Limits of Limited Government." *RP 50* (1988) 682–703.

Harbison, E. Harris. *The Age of Reformation.* Ithaca, NY: Cornell, 1955.

———. *The Christian Scholar in the Age of the Reformation.* New York: Charles Scribner's, 1956.

Heller, Henry. *The Conquest of Poverty: The Calvinist Revolt in Sixteenth Century France.* Leiden: Brill, 1986.

Hendrix, Scott. "Luther." In *The Cambridge Companion to Reformation Theology*, edited by David Bagchi et al, 39–56. Cambridge: Cambridge, 2004.

Háritier, Jean. "The Massacre of St. Bartholomew: Reason of State and Ideological Conflict." In *The French Wars of Religion,* edited by J.H.M. Salmon, 48–53. Boston: Heath, 1967.

Hesselink, I. John. *Calvin's Concept of the Law.* Allison Park, PA: Pickwick, 1992.

Holt, Mack P. *The French Wars of Religion, 1562–1629.* Cambridge: Cambridge, 1995.

Höpfl, Harro. *The Christian Polity of John Calvin.* Cambridge: Cambridge, 1982.

Hudson, Winthrop S. "Calvin a Source of Resistance Theory, and Therefore of Democracy." In *Calvin and Calvinism,* edited by Robert M. Kingdon et al, 15–24. Lexington, MA: Heath, 1970.

Hyma, Albert. *The Life of John Calvin.* Grand Rapids: Eerdmans, 1943.

Ingram, William. "Just War in Hugo Grotius' Rights of War and Peace." In *Peace, War and God's Justice*, edited by Thomas D. Parker et al, 71–79. Toronto: United Church Publishing, 1989.

James, Frank A. "A Late Medieval Parallel in Reformation Thought: *Gemina Praedestinatio* in Gregory of Rimini and Peter Martyr Vermigli." In *Via Augustini: Augustine in the Later Middle Ages, Renaissance and Reformation*, edited by Heiko A. Oberman et al, 158–88. Leiden: Brill, 1991.

Jeffreys, Derek S. "'It's a Miracle of God That There Is Any Common Weal among Us': Unfaithfulness and Disorder in John Calvin's Political Thought." *RP* (2000) 107–129.

Jinkins, Michael. "Theodore Beza: Continuity and Regression in the Reformed Tradition." *EQ* 64 (1992) 131–54.

Johnson, James Turner. *Ideology, Reason, and the Limitation of War: Religious and Secular Concepts.* Princeton: Princeton, 1975.

———. *Just War Tradition and the Restraint of War: A Moral and Historical Inquiry.* Princeton: Princeton, 1981.

———. *The Quest for Peace: Three Moral Traditions in Western Cultural History.* Princeton: Princeton, 1987.

Johnson, Merwyn S. "Calvin's Ethical Legacy." In *The Legacy of John Calvin*, edited by David Foxgrover, 63–83. Grand Rapids: CRC, 2000.

Jones, Archer. *The Art of War in the Western World.* Urbana and Chicago: University of Illinois, 1987.

Keddie, Gordon J. "Calvin on Civil Government." *SBET* 3 (1985) 23–35.

Keegan, John. *A History of Warfare.* New York: Random, 1993.

Keen, M. H. *The Laws of War in the Late Middle Ages.* London: Routledge; Toronto: University of Toronto, 1965.

Keen, Ralph. "The Limits of Power and Obedience in the Later Calvin." *CTJ* 27 (1992) 252–76.

Keillor, Steven J. *This Rebellious House: American History and the Truth of Christianity.* Downers Grove, IL: Intervarsity, 1996.

Kelly, Douglas F. *The Emergence of Liberty in the Modern World: The Influence of Calvin on Five Governments from the 16th through the 18th Centuries.* Phillipsburg, NJ: Presbyterian and Reformed, 1992.

———. "The Political Ideas of John Calvin as Reflected in His Sermons on 2 Samuel." *Evangel* 2 (1984) 11–15.

Kennedy, Thomas. "Can War Be Justified?" In *From Christ to the World: Introductory Readings in Christian Ethics*, edited by Wayne Boulton et al, 436–42. Grand Rapids: Eerdmans, 1994.

Kingdon, Robert M. *Adultery and Divorce in Calvin's Geneva.* Cambridge, MA and London: Harvard, 1995.

———. "Calvin and the Establishment of Consistory Discipline in Geneva: The Institution and the Men Who Directed It." *DRCH* 70 (1990) 158–72.

———. Calvin and the Family: The Work of the Consistory in Geneva." *PTR* 17 (1984) 5–18.

———. "Calvin and the Government of Geneva." In *Calvinus Ecclesiae Genevensis Custos,* edited by Wilhelm H. Neuser, 49–67. Frankfurt: Verlag Peter Lang, 1984.

———. "Calvin and 'Presbytery': the Geneva Company of Pastors." *PTR* 18 (1985) 43–55.

———. "Calvinism and Social Welfare." *CTJ* 17 (1982) 212–30.

———. "Calvin's Socio-Political Legacy: Collective Government, Resistance to Tyranny, Discipline." In *The Legacy of John Calvin,* edited by David Foxgrover, Grand Rapids: CRC Product Services, 2000.

———. "The Control of Morals by the Earliest Calvinists." In *Renaissance, Reformation, Resurgence,* edited by Peter De Klerk, 95–106. Grand Rapids: Calvin Theological Seminary, 1976.

———. "The Control of Morals in Calvin's Geneva." In *The Social History of the Reformation,* edited by Lawrence P. Buck et al, 3–16. Columbus: Ohio State, 1972.

———. "The First Expression of Theodore Beza's Political Ideas." *ARG* 46 (1955) 88–100.

———. "Foreward." In *Shapers of Religious Traditions in Germany, Switzerland, Poland, 1560–1600,* edited by Jill Raitt, vii–x. New Haven and London: Yale, 1981.

———. "The Function of Law in the Political Thought of Peter Martyr Vermigli." In *Reformatio Perrennis: Essays on Calvin and the Reformation,* edited by Brian Gerrish, 159–72. Pittsburgh: Pickwick, 1981.

———. "International Calvinism." In *Handbook of European History, 1400–1600,* edited by Thomas A. Brady et al, 229–47. Grand Rapids: Eerdmans, 1995.

———. *Myths about the St. Bartholomew's Day Massacres, 1572–1576.* Cambridge, MA and London: Harvard, 1988.

———. "Peter Martyr Vermigli and the Marks of the True Church." In *Continuity and Discontinuity in Church History,* edited by F. Forrestor Church et al, 198–214. Leiden: Brill, 1979.

———. "The Political Resistance of the Calvinists in France and the Low Countries." *CH* 27 (1958) 220–33.

———. "The Political Thought of Peter Martyr Vermigli." In *Peter Martyr Vermigli and Italian Reform,* edited by Joseph C. McClelland, 121–39. Waterloo, ONT: Wilfrid Laurier, 1980.

———. "Was the Protestant Reformation a Revolution? The Case of Geneva." In *Transition and Revolution: Problems and Issues of European Renaissance and Reformation History,* edited by Robert M. Kingdon, 53–77. Minneapolis: Burgess, 1974.

Kittelson, James M. *Luther the Reformer: The Story of the Man and His Career.* Minneapolis: Augsburg, 1986.

Klempa, William. "John Calvin on Natural Law." In *John Calvin and the Church,* edited by Timothy George, 72–95. Louisville: Westminster/John Knox, 1990.

———. "War and Peace in Puritan Thought." In *Peace, War and God's Justice,* edited by Thomas D. Parker et al, 81–103. Toronto: United Church, 1989.

Knudsen, Robert D. "Calvinism as a Cultural Force." In *John Calvin: His Influence in the Western World*, edited by W. Stanford Reid, 11–29. Grand Rapids: Zondervan, 1982.

Köhler, Walther. *Zürcher Ehegericht und Genfer Konsistorium.* Leipzig: Von M. Heinsius Nachfolger, 1932.

Kuyper, Abraham. "Freedom." In *Abraham Kuyper: A Centennial Reader.* Edited by James D. Bratt, 317–22. Grand Rapids: Eerdmans, 1988.

———. *Lectures on Calvinism.* Grand Rapids: Eerdmans, 1931.

Labrousse, Elisabeth. *Bayle.* Translated by Denys Potts. Oxford and New York: Oxford, 1983.

———. "Calvinism in France, 1598–1685." In *International Calvinism, 1541–1715,* edited by Menna Prestwich, 285–314. Oxford: Clarendon, 1985.

Lane, Anthony N.S. "The City of God: Church and State in Geneva." In *God and Caesar*, 42–53. London: British Evangelical Council, 1973.

———. *John Calvin: Student of the Church Fathers.* Grand Rapids: Baker, 1999.

Larson, Mark J. "A Champion of the Original American Republic: The Political Thought of James Thornwell." *JPH* 82 (2004) 258–70.

———. "John Calvin and Genevan Presbyterianism." *WTJ* 60 (1998) 43–69.

Leith, John H. "Calvin's Theological Method and the Ambiguity in His Theology." In *Reformation Studies: Essays in Honor of Roland H. Bainton*, edited by Franklin H. Littell, 106–14, 265–66. Richmond: John Knox, 1962.

———. *Introduction to the Reformed Tradition.* Rev. ed. Atlanta: John Knox, 1981.

Linder, Robert D. "John Calvin, Pierre Viret and the State." In *Calvin and the State*, edited by Peter De Klerk, 171–85. Grand Rapids: Calvin Studies Society, 1993.

———. "Pierre Viret's Concept of a Just War." *AUSS* 22 (1984) 213–30.

Linse, Eugene. "Beza and Melanchthon on Political Obligation." *CTM* 41 (1970) 27–35.

Little, David. *Religion, Order, and Law: A Study in Pre-Revolutionary England.* Chicago: University of Chicago Press, 1984.

Lloyd, H.A. "Calvin and the Duty of Guardians to Resist." *JEH* 32 (1981) 65–67.

Loetscher, Lefferts A. *A Brief History of the Presbyterians.* Philadelphia: Westminster, 1978.

Logan, Samuel T. "New England Puritans and the State." In *Theonomy: A Reformed Critique*, edited by William S. Barker et al, 353–84. Grand Rapids: Zondervan, 1990.

———. "Where Have All the Tulips Gone?" *WTJ* 50 (1988) 1–26.

Lucas, Henry S. "The Calvinist Revolt." In *The Renaissance and the Reformation*, 581–611. New York: Harper, 1960.

Luscombe, D.E. "The State of Nature and the Origin of the State." In *The Cambridge History of Later Medieval Philosophy*, edited by Norman Kretzmann et al., 757–70. Cambridge: Cambridge, 1982.

Mackinnon, James. *Calvin and the Reformation.* London: Longmans, 1936.

Manetsch, Scott M. *Theodore Beza and the Quest for Peace in France, 1572–1598.* Leiden: Brill, 2000.

Marsden, George. *The American Revolution.* Grand Rapids: The National Union of Christian Schools, 1973.

Maruyama, Tadataka. *The Ecclesiology of Theodore Beza.* Geneva: Droz, 1978.

McCoy, Charles, and J. Wayne Baker. *Fountainhead of Federalism: Heinrich Bullinger and the Covenantal Tradition.* Louisville: Westminster/John Knox, 1991.

McDonald, Forrest. *Novus Ordo Seclorum: The Intellectual Origins of the Constitution.* Lawrence, KS: University Press of Kansas, 1985.

———. *The Presidency of George Washington.* American Presidency. Lawrence, KS: University Press of Kansas, 1974.

McDonald, Forrest, and Ellen Shapiro McDonald. "Eighteenth-Century Warfare as a Cultural Ritual." In *Requiem: Variations on Eighteenth-Century Themes*, 39–58. Lawrence, KS: University Press of Kansas, 1988.

McGoldrick, James E. *Luther's English Connection.* Milwaukee: Northwestern, 1979.

McGrath, Alister. *A Life of John Calvin: A Study in the Shaping of Western Culture.* Oxford: Basil Blackwell, 1990.

———. *Reformation Thought: An Introduction.* 2nd ed. Oxford: Basil Blackwell, 1993.

McIlwain, Charles Howard. *The Growth of Political Thought in the West: From the Greeks to the End of the Middle Ages.* New York: Macmillan, 1932.

McKee, Elsie A. "Calvin and His Colleagues as Pastors: Some New Insights into the Collegial Ministry of Word and Sacraments." In *Calvinus Praeceptor Ecclesiae,* edited by Herman J. Selderhuis, 9–42. Geneva: Droz, 2004.

———. "Calvin's Teaching on the Elder Illuminated by Exegetical History." In *John Calvin and the Church,* edited by Timothy George, 147–155. Louisville: Westminster/John Knox, 1990.

———. *Elders and the Plural Ministry: The Role of Exegetical History in Illuminating John Calvin's Theology.* Geneva: Droz, 1988.

———. "The Offices of Elders and Deacons in the Classical Reformed Tradition." In *Major Themes in the Reformed Tradition*, edited by Donald K. McKim, 344–53. Grand Rapids: Eerdmans, 1992.

McKim, Donald K. "War and Peace in Calvin's Theology." In *Peace, War, and God's Justice,* edited by Thomas D. Parker et al, 53–69. Toronto: United Church Publishing, 1989.

McLelland, Joseph C. "Peter Martyr Vermigli: Scholastic or Humanist?" In *Peter Martyr Vermigli and Italian Reform,* edited by Joseph C. McClelland, 141–51. Waterloo, ONT: Wilfrid Laurier, 1980.

McNair, Philip. *Peter Martyr in Italy: An Anatomy of Apostasy.* Oxford: Oxford, 1967.

McNeill, John T. "Calvin and Civil Government." In *Readings in Calvin's Theology,* edited by Donald K. McKim, 260–74. Grand Rapids: Baker, 1984.

———. "Calvin Preferred Representative Democracy." In *Calvin and Calvinism*, edited by Robert M. Kingdon et al, 30–35. Lexington, MA: Heath, 1970.

———. *The History and Character of Calvinism*. Oxford: Oxford, 1954.

———. "John Calvin: Doctor Ecclesiae." In *Readings in Calvin's Theology*, edited by Donald K. McKim, 11–20. Grand Rapids: Baker, 1984.

Merriman, Roger B. *Suleiman the Magnificent, 1520–1566*. New York: Cooper Square, 1966.

Mesnard, Pierre. *L'essor de la Philosophie Politique au XVI Siecle*. Paris: Librairie Philosophique J. Vrin, 1951.

Miller, Gregory J. "Fighting Like a Christian: The Ottoman Advance and the Development of Luther's Doctrine of Just War." In *Caritas et Reformatio: Essays on Church and Society in Honor of Carter Lindberg*, edited by David M. Whitford, 41–57. Saint Louis: Concordia, 2002.

Miller, Richard B. *Interpretations of Conflict: Ethics, Pacifism, and the Just-War Tradition*. Chicago and London: University of Chicago, 1991.

Milner, Benjamin C. *Calvin's Doctrine of the Church*. Leiden: Brill, 1970.

Monter, E. William. *Calvin's Geneva*. New York: John Wiley, 1967.

———. "The Consistory of Geneva." *BHR* 38 (1976) 467–84.

———. "Crime and Punishment in Calvin's Geneva, 1562." *ARH* 64 (1973) 281–87.

———. "Daily Life and the Reformed Church." In *The Reformation*, edited by Pierre Chaunu, 244–52. New York: St. Martin's, 1990.

Morgan, Edmund S. *The Puritan Dilemma: The Story of John Winthrop*. Boston and Toronto: Little, 1958.

Muller, Richard A. "Biblical Interpretation in the Era of the Reformation: the View from the Middle Ages." In *Biblical Interpretation in the Era of the Reformation,* edited by Richard A. Muller et al, 3–22. Grand Rapids and Cambridge, UK: Eerdmans, 1996.

———. "Biblical Interpretation in the 16th and 17th Centuries." In *Historical Handbook of Major Biblical Interpreters,* edited by Donald K. McKim, 123–52. Downers Grove, IL: Intervarsity, 1998.

———. *Christ and the Decree: Christology and Predestination in Reformed Theology from Calvin to Perkins*. Durham, NC: Labyrinth, 1986.

———. *The Unaccommodated Calvin: Studies in the Foundation of a Theological Tradition*. New York and Oxford: Oxford, 2000.

Munck, Thomas. *Seventeenth Century Europe: State, Conflict and the Social Order in Europe, 1598–1700*. London: Macmillan, 1990.

Mundey, Paul. "John Calvin and Anabaptists on War." *BLT* 23 (1978) 239–47.

Murdock, Graeme. *Beyond Calvin: The Intellectual, Political and Cultural World of Europe's Churches, c. 1540–1620*. New York: Palgrave Macmillan, 2004.

Naphy, William G. *Calvin and the Consolidation of the Genevan Reformation*. Manchester and New York: Manchester, 1994.

———. "Church and State in Calvin's Geneva." In *Calvin and the Church*, edited by David Foxgrover, 13–28. Grand Rapids: CRC, 2002.

Nauert, Charles. *Humanism and the Culture of Renaissance Europe*. Cambridge: Harvard, 1995.

Neale, J.E. *The Age of Catherine de Medici*. New York and Evanston: Harper, 1962.

Niebuhr, H. Richard. *Christ and Culture*. New York: Harper, 1951.

Oberman, Heiko A. "John Calvin: The Mystery of His Impact." In *Calvin Studies VI*, edited by John M. Leith, 1–14. Davidson, NC: Calvin Colloquium, 1992.

Old, Hughes Oliphant. "Bullinger and the Scholastic Works on Baptism, A Study in the History of Christian Worship." In *Heinrich Bullinger, 1504–1575*, edited by Ulrich Gäbler et al, 191–207. Zurich: Theologischer Verlag, 1975.

Olson, Jeannine. "The Bourse Française: Deacons and Social Welfare in Calvin's Geneva." *PTR* 15 (1982) 18–24.

———. "Calvin as Pastor-Administrator During the Reformation in Geneva." *PTR* 14 (1981) 10–17.

———. "Reformation and Revolution in Calvin's Geneva." *Halcyon* 7 (1985) 93–103.

———. "A Response to 'Calvin's Socio-Political Legacy: Collective Government, Resistance to Tyranny, and Discipline.'" In *The Legacy of John Calvin*, edited by David Foxgrover, 124–29. Grand Rapids: CRC, 2000.

———. "Response to 'John Calvin, Pierre Viret and the State.'" In *Calvin and the State*, edited by Peter De Klerk, 187–88. Grand Rapids: Calvin Studies Society, 1993.

Opitz, Peter. "Bullinger's *Decades*: Instruction in Faith and Conduct." In *Architect of Reformation: An Introduction to Heinrich Bullinger, 1504–1575*, edited by Bruce Gordon et al, 101–16. Grand Rapids: Baker, 2004.

Packer, James I. "The Faith of the Protestants." In *Eerdman's Handbook to the History of Christianity*, edited by Tim Dowley, 374–75. Grand Rapids: Eerdmans, 1977.

———. *A Quest for Godliness: The Puritan Vision of the Christian Life*. Wheaton, IL: Crossway, 1990.

Parker, T.H.L. *Calvin: An Introduction to His Thought*. Louisville: Westminster/John Knox, 1995.

———. *Calvin's Old Testament Commentaries*. Edinburgh: T. & T. Clark, 1986.

———. *Calvin's Preaching*. Louisville: Westminster/John Knox, 1992.

———. *The Doctrine of the Knowledge of God: A Study in the Theology of John Calvin*. Rev. ed. Grand Rapids: Eerdmans, 1959.

———. *John Calvin*. Trian, Batavia, and Sydney: Lion, 1975.

Paskins, Barrie, and Michael Dockrill. *The Ethics of War*. Minneapolis: University of Minnesota, 1979.

Pfeffer, Leo. *Church, State, and Freedom*. Revised. Boston: Beacon, 1967.

Pinette, G. L. "Freedom in Huguenot Doctrine." *ARG* 50 (1959) 200–234.

Prestwich, Menna. "The Changing Face of Calvinism." In *International Calvinism 1541–1715*, edited by Menna Prestwich, 1–14. Oxford: Clarendon, 1985.

Raath, Andries. "Covenant and the Christian Community: Bullinger and the Relationship between Church and Magistracy in Early Cape Settlement (1652–1708)." *SCJ* 33 (2002) 999–1019.

Raath, Andries, and Shaun de Freitas. "Theologico-Political Federalism: The Office of Magistracy and the Legacy of Heinrich Bullinger (1504–1575)." *WTJ* 63 (2001) 285–304.

Ramsey, Paul. *War and the Christian Conscience: How Shall Modern War Be Conducted Justly?* Durham, NC: Duke, 1961.

Raynal, Charles E. "The Place of the Academy in Calvin's Polity." In *John Calvin and the Church*, edited by Timothy George, 120–34. Louisville: Westminster/John Knox, 1990.

Reid, James. *Memoirs of the Westminster Divines*. Edinburgh: Banner of Truth, 1982.

Reid, W. Stanford. "The Impact of Calvinism on Sixteenth Century Culture." *IRB* 10 (1967) 3–10.

———. "John Calvin, Lawyer and Legal Reformer." In *Through Christ's Word*, edited by W. Robert Godfrey et al, 149–64. Phillipsburg, NJ: Presbyterian and Reformed, 1985.

———. "John Calvin, Pastoral Theologian." *RTR* 42 (1982) 65–73.

———. "John Knox and the Scottish Reformation." In *Geneva to Geelong: The Ideas and Influence of John Calvin,* edited by Gordon Oosterman, 45–57. Grand Rapids: The National Union of Christian Schools, 1974.

———. "John Knox: The First of the Monarchomachs?" In *The Covenant Connection,* edited by Daniel J. Elazar, 119–41. New York: Lexington Books, 2000.

———. "The Transmission of Calvinism in the Sixteenth Century." In *John Calvin: His Influence in the Western World,* edited by W. Stanford Reid, 33–52. Grand Rapids: Zondervan, 1982.

Rice, Eugene F., and Anthony Grafton. *The Foundations of Early Modern Europe, 1460–1559.* 2nd ed. New York and London: Norton, 1994.

Riley-Smith, Jonathan. "Christian Violence and the Crusades." In *The Oxford History of the Crusades,* edited by Jonathan Riley-Smith, 1–14. Oxford: Oxford, 2002.

Roget, Amée. *L'Église et l'État à Genève du temps de Calvin.* Geneva: J. Jullien, 1867.

Russell, Frederick H. *The Just War in the Middle Ages.* Cambridge: Cambridge, 1975.

Salmon, J.H.M. *Society in Crisis: France in the Sixteenth Century.* New York: St. Martin's, 1975.

Sanders, Thomas G. "The Calvinist Origins of Transformationism." In *The Protestant Concepts of Church and State,* 225–34. New York: Holt, Rinehart and Winston, 1964.

Sap, John W. *Paving the Way for Revolution: Calvinism and the Struggle for a Democratic Constitutional State.* Amsterdam: UV Uitgeverij, 2001.

Schreiner, Susan E. *The Theater of His Glory: Nature and the Natural Order in the Thought of John Calvin.* Durham, NC: Labyrinth, 1991.

Singer, C. Gregg. "Calvin and the Social Order or Calvin as a Social and Economic Statesman." In *John Calvin: Contemporary Prophet,* edited by Jacob T. Hoogstra, 227–41. Grand Rapids: Baker, 1959.

———. *John Calvin: His Roots and Fruits.* Greenville, SC: A Press, 1989.

———. *A Theological Interpretation of American History.* 3rd ed. Greenville, SC: A Press, 1994.

Skinner, Quentin. *The Foundations of Modern Political Thought.* 2 vols. Cambridge: Cambridge, 1978.

Smith, William K. *Calvin's Ethics of War.* Annapolis: Academic Fellowship, 1972.

Smither, James R. "The St. Bartholomew's Day Massacre and Images of Kingship in France: 1572–1574." *SCJ* 22 (1991) 27–46.

Spitz, Lewis W. *The Protestant Reformation: 1517–1559*. New York: Harper, 1985.

Spykman, Gordon J. "The Principled Pluralist Position." In *God and Politics: Four Views on the Reformation of Civil Government*, edited by Gary Scott Smith, 78–99. Phillipsburg, NJ: Presbyterian and Reformed, 1989.

Stauffer, Richard. "La Réforme Calvinienne." In *Histoire des religions*, 944–53. Paris: Éditions Gallimard, 1972.

———. *L'Humanité de Calvin*. Neuchâtel: Delachaux et Niestlé, 1964.

Steinmetz, David C. *Calvin in Context*. New York and Oxford: Oxford, 1995.

———. "The Scholastic Calvin." In *Protestant Scholasticism: Essays in Reassessment*, edited by Carl R. Trueman, 16–30. Carlisle: Paternoster, 1999.

———. "The Superiority of Pre-Critical Exegesis." *TT* 37 (1980–81) 27–38.

Stephenson, Carl. *Mediæval History: Europe from the Second to the Sixteenth Century*. Rev. ed. New York and London: Harper, 1943.

Stevenson, William R. "Calvin and Political Issues." In *The Cambridge Companion to John Calvin*, edited by Donald K. McKim, 173–87. Cambridge: Cambridge, 2004.

Strohl, Jane E. "Ministry in the Middle Ages and the Reformation." In *Called and Ordained*, edited by Todd Nichol et al, 35–48. Minneapolis: Fortress, 1990.

Sunshine, Glenn S. "Reformed Theology and the Origins of Synodical Polity: Calvin, Beza and the Gallican Confession." In *Later Calvinism: International Perspectives*, edited by William Fred Graham, 141–58. Kirksville, MO: Sixteenth Century Journal, 1994.

Tanoue, Masanaru. "An Introduction to Calvin's Political Thought." *JLPS* 31 (1996) 319–49.

Taylor, George A. "John Calvin, the Teacher: The Correlation between Instruction and Nurture within Calvin's Concept of Communion." Ph.D. diss., Duke University, 1953.

Thompson, Bard. *Humanists and Reformers: A History of the Renaissance and Reformation*. Grand Rapids and Cambridge: Eerdmans, 1996.

Thompson, Ernest T. *Presbyterians in the South*. Vol. 1. Richmond, VA: John Knox, 1963.

Thompson, John L. "Patriarchs, Polygamy, and Private Resistance: John Calvin and Others on Breaking God's Rules." *SCJ* 25 (1994) 3–27.

Thompson, John L. "The Survival of Allegorical Argumentation in Peter Martyr Vermigli's Old Testament Exegesis." In *Biblical Interpretation in the Era of the Reformation,* edited by Richard A. Muller et al, 255–71. Grand Rapids and Cambridge, UK: Eerdmans, 1996.

Torrance, Thomas F. "The Eldership in the Reformed Church." *SJT* 37 (1984) 503–18.

———. *Hermeneutics of John Calvin.* Edinburgh: Scottish Academic Press, 1988.

Vos, Arvin. *Aquinas, Calvin, and Contemporary Thought: A Critique of Protestant Views on the Thought of Thomas Aquinas.* Grand Rapids: Eerdmans, 1985.

Walker, Williston. *John Calvin: The Organiser of Reformed Protestantism, 1509–1564.* New York and London: G. P. Putnam's, 1906.

Wallace, Ronald S. *Calvin, Geneva and the Reformation: A Study of Calvin as Social Reformer, Churchman, Pastor and Theologian.* Edinburgh: Scottish Academic Press, 1988.

———. *Calvin's Doctrine of the Word and Sacrament.* Edinburgh: Oliver and Boyd, 953.

Walton, Robert C. *Zwingli's Theocracy.* Toronto: University of Toronto, 1967.

Walzer, Michael. *Just and Unjust Wars: A Moral Argument with Historical Illustrations.* New York: Basic Books, 1977.

———. *The Revolution of the Saints: A Study in the Origins of Radical Politics.* Cambridge, MA: Harvard, 1965.

Watt, Jeffrey R. "Calvinism, Childhood, and Education: The Evidence from the Genevan Consistory." *SCJ* 33 (2002) 439–56.

———. "Women and the Consistory in Calvin's Geneva." *SCJ* 24 (1983) 429–39.

Wendel, François. *Calvin: Origins and Development of His Religious Thought.* Translated by Philip Mairet. London: William Collins, 1963. Reprint, Grand Rapids: Baker, 1997.

———. *L'Église de Strasbourg, sa constitution et son organization, 1532–1535.* Paris: PUF, 1942.

Whitford, David W. "Luther's Political Encounters." In *The Cambridge Companion to Martin Luther,* edited by Donald K. McKim, 179–91. Cambridge: Cambridge, 2003.

———. *Tyranny and Resistance: The Magdeburg Confession and the Lutheran Tradition.* Saint Louis: Concordia, 2001.

Witte, John. "Moderate Religious Liberty in the Theology of John Calvin." *CTJ* 31 (1996) 359–403.

———. *Religion and the American Constitutional Experiment.* 2nd ed. Boulder, CO: Westview, 2005.

Wolin, Sheldon S. *Politics and Vision: Continuity and Innovation in Western Political Thought.* Boston: Little, 1960.

Wright, David F. "War in a Church-Historical Perspective." *EQ* 57 (1985) 133–61.

Yang, Nak Heong. "Reformed Social Ethics and the Korean Church." PhD diss., Fuller Theological Seminary, 1993.

Yardeni, Myriam. "French Calvinist Political Thought, 1534–1715." In *International Calvinism, 1541–1715,* edited by Menna Prestwich, 315–37. Oxford: Clarendon, 1985.

Subject/Name Index

absolutism, 91–92
Adams, John, 96
Alciato, Andrea, 16
Alexander of Hales, 25
Allen, Ethan, 98
alliances, 38
Althusius, Johannes, 53
ambassadors, 76
ambush, 37–38
anarchy, 93
Aquinas, Thomas, 24–27, 60–61, 67–69, 72–74, 84–85
archers, 36
artillery, 36
Augustine, 25–27, 67, 72–73

Bernard, Jacques, 13
Beza, Theodore, 53–57, 62–65, 70–71, 83
bishops, 10–11
brevitas et facilitas, 30
Bucer, Martin, 56–57
Buchanan, George, 103
Bullinger, Henry, 27–29, 49–51, 65, 71–72, 78–79

capital punishment, 84–88
Cavaliers, 89
cavalry, 36
chariots, 36
Charles I of England, 89
Charles VIII of France, 36

Charles IX of France, 53
Christian commonwealth, 68–72, 86–87
Christian II of Denmark, 62
church discipline, 5–6
Cicero, 45, 75
Clement VII, Pope, 21
collective government, 12–14
Company of Pastors, 12–13
conservatism, xv–xvii
consistory, 4–7, 12–14, 81–82
Constitutional Convention, 94–96
Continental Army, 89
Cop, Michael, 13
Cotton, John, 94
crossbows, 35

de Coligny, Gaspard, 53
defensive war, 68–72
democracy, 93–95
de Montfort, Simon, 60
de Pisan, Christine, 60
deposition, 62–65
diplomacy, 76, 80
disputation, 73–74
doctors of canon law, 4
Drogheda, 50
Dutch Rebellion, 89

Ecclesiastical Ordinances, 4–7
Edict of Nantes, 57
egalitarianism, 95–96

Subject/Name Index

elders, 13–16
electors, 95
England, 64
English Civil War, 51, 89
Erastianism, xvii, 5, 102–03
established church, 83–84
Estates-General, 58–59, 63–65

faction, 94
Federalist, The, 94–95
First Amendment, 82–83
First Crusade, 20
franchise, 92–93, 96–97

Geneva, 18–19, 84–87
Gouge, William, 41–42
George III of England, 90
Gregory IX, Pope, 35

harquebusiers, 36
Hebrew exegesis, 82
Henry of Navarre, 53
heresy, 84–88
holy commonwealth, 84
holy days, 68
holy war, 20–21, 32–33, 41–43, 69
horses, 38–39
Huguenots, 53

Infantry, 36, 49
inferior magistrates, 55–57
Institutes, 30, 73–74

James I of England, 98
Jerusalem, 20
Jewish ghettos, 19
John of England, 60
John of Salisbury, 37, 67, 85
judges, 88
Julius II, Pope, 21

jus ad bellum, 32, 34, 66–80
jus in bello, 34, 43–51
just cause, 24, 67–72
Justinian Code, 85

knights, 36, 49
Knox, John, 19
Kuyper, Abraham, 101

last resort, 75–80
law, 52–53, 103
legal scholarship, 16
Lepanto, Battle of, 20
l'Estoile, Pierre de, 16
liberty, 68–69, 101
Lord's Supper, 84
Luther, Martin, 20–21, 56, 62–67, 72, 77–78

Madison, James, 82–83, 94–96
Magna Carta, 60
Marguerite of Valois, 53
Maryland Act Concerning Religion, 87
Massachusetts Bay, 94
ministerial education, 13
Mohacs, Battle of, 43–44
monarchy, 90–92
Muslims, 20
Myconius, Oswald, 102

nobles, 58–59
North, Frederick, 90

Oecolampadius, Johannes, 4–5
Ottoman Turks, 43–44

Paine, Thomas, 98
papacy, 10
Papal States, 7

parliamentary resistance, 55–59, 81–82
pastoral theology, 7–11, 81–82
Peace of God, 35
Philip IV of France, 58
Philip II of Spain, 89
pike men, 36
populares magistratus, 57–59, 89
prayer, 54
preaching, 22
Presbyterian polity, 102
Presbyterian Rebellion, 89–90
president, 95
priests, 11
prince, 20–33, 88
prisoners of war, 48–49

regalian bishops, 3–4
religious freedom, 84
representatives, 95
republicanism, 17–18, 81, 90–99, 102–3
right intention, 24–25, 72–75
Rutherford, Samuel, 103

scholastic methodology, 28–31, 73–74
Scotch-Irish, 98
Second Continental Congress, 89, 99
Second Lateran Council, 35
sedition, 93–94
Seigneury, 5, 17
senators, 95
separation of church and state, 2, 81–82
servant avenger, 54
Servetus, Michael, 6–7, 85–87
siege machines, 35
siege warfare, 44–46

sin, 39–40
single-sphere doctrine, 102
Small Council, 7, 14, 17, 85–86
social reform, 4, 18–19
soldiers, 78
Spanish Inquisition, 83
St. Bartholomew massacres, 53
Suleyman, 43–44
surgery metaphor, 78–79
Swiss Reformation, xvi–xvii

tactics, 37–38
theocracy, 1–3, 17–19
theonomy, 45–46
Toulouse, 86–87
Trinity, 87
two-sphere doctrine, 2–7, 81–82
tyranny, 52–59, 89–93

Urban II, Pope, 20

Valois, House of, 36
Vermigli, Peter Martyr, 29–32, 49, 61–62, 65, 71–72, 79–80
Viret, Pierre, 13

Wars of Religion, 56–57
Washington, George, 89
weapons, 36–41
Westminster Assembly, 102

www.ingramcontent.com/pod-product-compliance
Lightning Source LLC
Chambersburg PA
CBHW072150160426
43197CB00012B/2319